IMPRESSIONISM

Isabel Kuhl

IMPRESSIONISM

A Celebration of Light

PaRragon

Bath · New York · Singapore · Hong Kong · Cologne · Delhi · Melbourne

CONTENTS

PARIS IN THE MIDDLE OF THE NINETEENTH CENTURY: HISTORY PAINTERS AND REBELS

How convenient that there is a concise definition for everything! What, then, was the defining feature of Impressionist painting? What characterized the Impressionists' group exhibitions that united Monet, Degas, Manet, and Renoir? "It's perfectly simple," explained Georges Rivière (*Landschaft im Licht*), one of their champions and later, Renoir's biographer, "they just hung the word 'Impressionists' on the door of their exhibition." In 1877, when the eighteen participants referred to themselves at their third show as "Impressionists," this was literally true. However, the unanimity shown on this occasion was short-lived.

Not only did the exhibition title change with each subsequent exhibition, so too did the venue and the line-up of exhibiting artists. Edgar Degas rejected the word "Impressionist" as a description of his works. Claude Monet came to terms with it but regretted being the reason, thanks to his famous painting *Impression: Sunrise* (ill. p.9), "that the name was given to a group most of whose members had nothing impressionistic about them" (*Impressionist Masterpieces*). The situation was apparently not as clear as Rivière had described it. What, then, did the word "Impressionists" actually mean?

Cham, real name Amédée Charles Henri de Noé, cartoon published in *Le Charivari*, April 28, 1877. Lithograph, Bibliothèque Nationale, Paris.

PAGES 6–7
Claude Monet, *Impression: Sunrise* (detail), 1873.
Oil on canvas, 19 x 24¾ in. (48 x 63 cm). Musée Marmottan, Paris.

"Claude Monet has succeeded in capturing the fleeting impression neglected by his predecessors or deemed by them to be impossible to depict with the brush.... By no longer merely painting the immobile and unchanging aspect of a landscape but also the fleeting sensory impressions conveyed to him by its atmosphere and mood, Monet creates an incredibly vivid and powerful impression of the observed scene. His pictures really do convey impressions."

Théodore Duret

A glance at their work nevertheless reveals a number of common features: landscapes and cityscapes are filled with sunshine, shimmering light, and air. The leading role is played by everyday, modern life, whether that is work or leisure time spent at the ballet, in cafés, or on the banks of the

Claude Monet, *Impression: Sunrise*, 1873.
Oil on canvas, 19 x 24¾ in. (48 x 63 cm). Musée Marmottan, Paris.

Seine. The paintings of Renoir, Pissarro, or Monet seldom tell stories. Instead they capture moments, impressions. When the emphasis is on the individual's own perception and the object is to depict what the eye sees rather than what the head knows, everything suddenly becomes worthy of being the subject of a work of art—clouds of smoke in a station, a garden flooded with light, boating on the River Seine, a boulevard full of people, or a snow-covered field.

These painters adapted their technique and composition to suit the moment: In some cases the center of the canvas remains empty or figures are cut off by the edge of the picture; in others, objects are often merely hinted at with a few brief brushstrokes. Many of these paintings resemble sketches and have indeed been created rapidly and "on location"; most Impressionists preferred to paint outdoors rather than in the studio. It is these different artistic tendencies rather than that of a specific clear style that the term "Impressionism" denotes.

Works like Monet's *Impression: Sunrise* (which depicts a harbor in the early morning light) provoked a hostile response from the majority of critics and the public. This is difficult to understand today, given that our enthusiasm for Impressionist paintings has continued unabated for decades and new records are continually being set by exhibitions and auctions in terms of visitor numbers and prices realized. Notwithstanding this, many contemporaries reacted to these "impressions" with shock,

PAGES 10–11
Henri Fantin-Latour, *Homage to Delacroix*, 1864.
Oil on canvas, 63 x 98½ in. (160 x 250 cm). Musée d'Orsay, Paris.

Various writers and artists of the day gather around the portrait of their revered Delacroix. Seated from left to right: art critic Edmond Duranty, Henri Fantin-Latour (holding palette), writers Jules Champfleury and Charles Baudelaire; standing from left to right: painters Louis Cordier, Alphonse Legros, James Abbott McNeill Whistler, Édouard Manet, Félix Bracquemond, and Albert de Balleroy.

Philippe Benoist and Eugène Guérard, *Paris, 1855 Industrial Exhibition:*
The Palais de l'Industrie and the Champs-Élysées.
Wood engraving of a contemporary lithograph.

indignation, and outrage, believing that such banal subjects had no place in art, especially when painted so clumsily and hastily. The works exhibited in 1877 struck the cartoonist Cham as so terrifying that he depicted them as a highly effective weapon of war (see ill. p.8).

The reasons why Impressionism became the specter of the middle classes are to be found in the circumstances out of which the movement developed. This book therefore starts with an examination of the French art world in the middle of the nineteenth century, focusing on the national institutions. The second half of the century was dominated by attempts to break free of the establishment straitjacket. Édouard Manet attempted to bring about a revolution from within the system while the Impressionists positioned themselves outside the art establishment and created their own market with their group exhibitions. The third and fourth chapters of this book focus on the individual directions that were taken and the artistic personalities and interactions between the painters and the public, collectors, critics, and dealers who developed during the 1870s and 1880s. To quote one contemporary critic, Philippe Burty, "They are like tiny fragments of universal life and the swift, colorful, subtle, and enchanting things reflected in them deserve to be taken seriously and celebrated" (*Impressionist Masterpieces*). The book's attention then turns to the Impressionists' successors and pacemakers, the Pointillists and Post-Impressionists. That the world of Impressionism, with all its contradictory impulses, was broad—and by no means a purely French phenomenon—is demonstrated in the final chapter.

THE UNIVERSAL EXHIBITION

The first World's Fair to be held in Paris opened its doors on May 15, 1855.

Four years before, London had set the ball rolling and now it was the turn of the French capital to dazzle. The latest technological and scientific discoveries were presented in the

newly built Palais de l'Industrie, a masterpiece of steel and glass (ill. pp.12–13), but art was also well represented at the International Exhibition. The works (including 5,000 paintings) of artists from twenty-eight countries were shown in the Palais des Beaux-Arts. Major retrospectives of French painters were staged, among them Jean-Auguste-Dominique Ingres (1780–1867), who exhibited in a separate room, and Eugène Delacroix (1798–1863), who was given a generous space in the central hall. The tone was thus set by the leading exponents of two different styles of painting of the first half of the century: Ingres the Classicist and Delacroix the Romantic and forerunner of Impressionism.

Ingres was already a living institution whose fame had spread throughout Europe. He and his many followers were devoted primarily to history painting (see ill. p.17). They portrayed scenes from ancient history, the Bible, and mythology. As well as prescribing *what* to paint, the history painters also laid down *how* to paint, deeming clear composition, well-delineated figures and objects, and barely visible brushstrokes

as appropriate for their exalted subject matter. Their aim was to educate. History paintings, they believed, should rouse, inform, and impart a sense of virtue and morality, most importantly in an official context. Their largest customer (and usually commissioner of the artwork) was the French State. For the painters in Ingres's circle, history painting may have meant a rather limited range of subjects, but it also meant the prospect of a good career.

Claude Monet painted *Impression: Sunrise* (ill. p.9) just six years after Ingres's death. The achievements of the Classicists had apparently passed him by. In Monet's canvases the heroic protagonist is the light, and virtually nothing can be clearly distinguished in his harbor view. Clear lines? Elaborate composition? Smooth brushwork? Wrong. Monet's enthusiasm for the Classicists was clearly limited. The work of Delacroix, on the other hand, had evidently left its mark.

Although Eugène Delacroix also painted historical scenes, he showed less enthusiasm than the Classicists for the stoical heroes of the past (ill. pp.14–15), instead filling his canvases

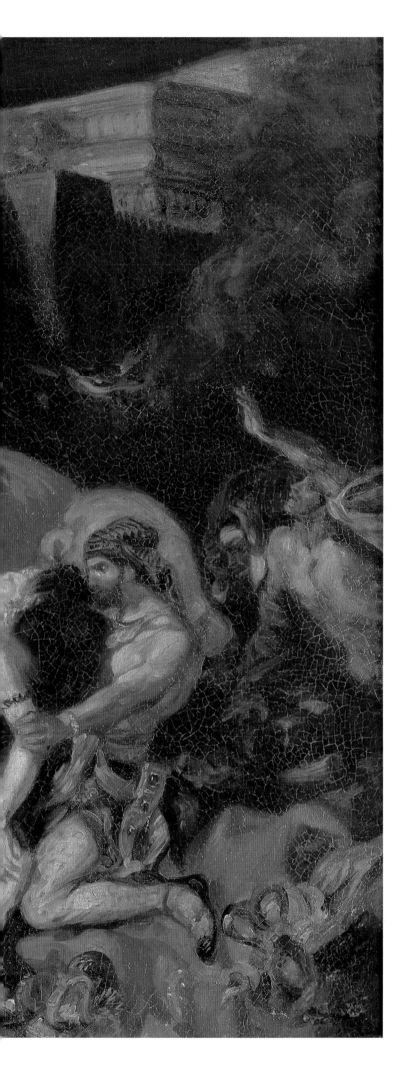

Eugène Delacroix, *The Death of Sardanapalus*, 1827.
Oil on canvas, 154¼ x 195¼ in. (392 x 496 cm). Musée du Louvre, Paris.

with fantastic and exotic subjects and occasionally turning to contemporary motifs. He used color and movement to depict inner conflict and the fate of individuals. The Classicists criticized what they perceived as a lack of draftsmanship, and others considered his subject matter excessively liberal. Only with the Universal Exhibition of 1855 did a turning point occur in the way the Romantic painter was perceived, and the rebel began suddenly to be seen as a colorist.

Delacroix's importance could no longer be overlooked, particularly as he enjoyed a good relationship with Prince Louis Napoleon (1822–91), a nephew of the emperor. Interpreters of art harnessed Delacroix to their own individual ends. Later generations, most importantly the Impressionists, came to see him as the great liberator. The esteem in which he was held was demonstrated by, among others, Henri Fantin-Latour, who painted his *Homage to Delacroix* one year after the painter's death, and included himself in the picture, palette in hand (ill. pp.10–11).

Delacroix was a model to other artists not only because of his independence from the state and critics, but also because of his enthusiasm for experimentation. He experimented with different color combinations and the visual effects they produced, favoring a lighter palette and even applying paint to white grounds. He also left visible brushstrokes instead of producing a smooth surface finish. These issues and techniques were later taken up vigorously by the Impressionists.

POLARIZATION

In 1855, Delacroix and Ingres saw their work presented under the same roof as equally valid. The Universal Exhibition polarized opinion and once again set the proponents of color (Delacroix) against the proponents of line (Ingres). By the time the official honors were handed out (a common practice at exhibitions of this kind), the pendulum had swung clearly one way. With Gérôme and Cabanel, the jury honored history painters who followed Ingres's style of painting. Thomas Couture (1815–79), meanwhile, who ran a big studio at the State École des Beaux-Arts, received a first-class medal. As his monumental masterpiece *The Romans of the Decadence* (ill. p.16) demonstrates, Couture also took his cue, in terms of both form and content, from antique art. The subject of this picture is based on a satire by the Roman poet Juvenal. While Couture's large-format works were better suited to public spaces (*The Romans of the Decadence*, for example, was acquired by the French State), other painters targeted the bourgeois public with genre paintings, which depicted scenes of everyday life and had been popular since the seventeenth century.

Thomas Couture, *The Romans of the Decadence*, 1847.
Oil on canvas, 185¾ x 304 in. (472 x 772 cm). Musée d'Orsay, Paris.

Ernest Meissonier (1815–91) was one of the most commercially successful artists of his day (ill. p.20). His small-format, highly detailed paintings of everyday scenes were better suited to the private market and proved extremely popular with the wealthy bourgeoisie. Meissonier did not leave the Universal Exhibition of 1855 empty-handed either, walking away with a Grande Médaille d'Honneur.

Around three-quarters of the works submitted to the exhibition were rejected by the jurors, including two large-scale paintings by Gustave Courbet (1819–77): *The Painter's Studio* and *A Burial at Ornans* (ill. pp.18–19). In the latter, which Courbet had presented to the Salon four years earlier, the artist lined up the inhabitants of his home village by the graveside in a kind of frieze. The somber palette and life-size depiction lent these figures a certain weight that, moreover, did not discriminate between peasants, mayor, and priests. Courbet had opened himself up to attack on a number of fronts: his handling (he liked to apply paint with palette knife rather than brush), his equal treatment of all the characters, and above all his chosen format (such monumental dimensions were reserved for history paintings while scenes of everyday and, particularly, peasant life were classified as "genre paintings"). Courbet saw things differently and, disregarding the established boundaries, described the work as a history painting. Contrary to Salon convention, he was convinced that painters should only paint their own lifetime and the things they had experienced. He depicted the everyday lives of ordinary people, workers, and the rural population without idealizing them. In an open letter of 1861 he wrote, "True artists are those who capture their epoch at the precise point to which the preceding ages have led them. In my opinion, painting is essentially a concrete art and can only consist of the depiction of *real, existing* things" (Wolf, see ill. p.22). Courbet's ideas, which he himself subsumed under the term "Realism," were to have major repercussions: modern times and everyday life, whether in the city or in the countryside, began to cast an increasingly strong spell over his fellow artists.

In 1855, however, Courbet was confronted by a very real problem: his exclusion from the Universal Exhibition. The decision of the jurors to reject a number of the fourteen works submitted by the artist provoked him to take a radical step. On the other side of Avenue Montaigne opposite the Palais des Beaux-Arts the painter mounted his own exhibition, parallel to the official one. For an admission charge of one franc, a fifth of the price of the Universal Exhibition, visitors were offered an alternative exhibition entitled "Le Réalisme." With this independent show, Courbet had created a new model for future generations of artists to follow.

The Universal Exhibition, then, endured without making any space available for modern art, which—other than that on display in Courbet's solo show—remained firmly in the studio. Instead, what shone forth from the Palais de l'Industrie was tradition in the shape of the established masters. Rather than looking to the future, the official exhibition was a celebration of the past. Jules Castagnary, a persistent critic of national art policy and later a director of the Beaux-Arts, was unable to identify any concept behind the exhibition other than a simple gathering of works from throughout the preceding half century, whose intention was surely not (he felt) to reiterate old positions ad nauseam. This retrogressive stance was commented on by a number of critics. What were the selection criteria? In charge of choosing works for the exhibition was a jury recruited primarily from the conservative camp. Indeed nearly all the jurors were professors at the venerable Académie des Beaux-Arts, and Classicism was indulged above all else (not least because of Ingres' enormous influence as an artist and teacher)

Jean-Auguste-Dominique Ingres, *The Source*, 1856.
Oil on canvas, 64¼ x 31½ in. (163 x 80 cm). Musée d'Orsay, Paris.

Delacroix "abandoned himself to his passionate notions and in so doing neglected that venerable foundation on which all depends: the art of drawing. Instead he has gone down the wrong track completely. Ingres, on the other hand, became great through draftsmanship. There's no getting away from the fact that should painting undergo a revival this century, Ingres will have made a major contribution to its renaissance by showing the clear-sighted the way to the summit."

Auguste de Gas to his son, Edgar, 1859

at this two-hundred-year-old institution that set the tone for French artistic life. Courbet was by no means the only artist whose ideas were at odds with those of the men in charge at the Académie des Beaux-Arts. Nevertheless, it was impossible to overestimate the Académie's influence over the country's artistic production and aesthetic preferences. Louis Napoleon had seen to this when he ascended the imperial throne as Napoleon III. Under his guidance the state monopoly over art,

a tradition whose roots lay in absolutist France, was revived. The Académie was responsible for organizing competitions and awarding medals. Its professors also made up the jury for the Salon exhibitions (see The Salon, pp.34–5).

From an economic point of view, participation in the regularly held Salon was essential. Apart from rare opportunities such as the Universal Exhibition, there was nowhere else for artists to exhibit their paintings. The influence

Gustave Courbet, *A Burial at Ornans*, 1849–50.
Oil on canvas, 124 x 263 in. (315 x 668 cm). Musée d'Orsay, Paris.

of the Académie also extended to the training of young artists and another of its responsibilities was therefore to appoint the teaching staff of the École des Beaux-Arts. The prevailing Classical outlook therefore percolated down to the state art school. Students at the École des Beaux-Arts started by perfecting their drawing technique. Not until they had mastered this were they allowed near any pigment—and then only to copy the works of old masters. Graduating from the École des Beaux-Arts was certainly a step in the direction of a career as an artist, but an even more effective route to success was to win the Prix de Rome.

This prize was awarded to the painter of what the exhibition jury judged to be the "best" history painting—a painting depicting a significant historical event, whether actual

or fictional—and it all but assured the winner of a successful career. History paintings were regarded as the most rigorous because they made intellectual demands of the artist. Next came genre painting. Here too it was considered important to depict the chosen subject using the most appropriate artistic means possible. Portraits and landscapes, by contrast, allowed painters to give their powers of observation free rein in an attempt to portray the sitter or view in a true-to-life manner—clearly no artistry required there! On which rung of the hierarchy of traditional subjects a painter belonged depended in part on how he saw himself. Ingres, for example, was in extremely high demand as a portraitist, but when a potential client knocked on his door looking for "Monsieur Ingres, the portrait painter," the door was slammed in his face….

Ernest Meissonier, *The Chess Players*, 1856.
Oil on panel, 10½ x 8½ in. (27 x 21.6 cm). Hamburger Kunsthalle, Germany.

EN PLEIN AIR

Although this view of landscape painting was well established, the genre enjoyed growing popularity during the first half of the century—among artists and collectors alike. From 1816 forward, the Salon jury was even prepared to award the Prix de Rome to painters of historical landscapes, albeit not natural landscapes in the sense of depictions of real events in nature but, as the name suggests, landscapes conceived and executed in the studio. These historical landscapes were generally Italianate, featuring a balanced color scheme and harmonious composition and not infrequently dotted with ruins. Some three decades later, Count Nieuwerkerke, the conservative superintendent of fine arts, described landscape painting as "the painting of democrats, of men who don't change their linen and who mean to force themselves on polite society. This art displeases and disgusts me" (Rewald).

During the Second Empire, landscape painters were regarded by the government as opponents of the regime and the growth in popularity of landscape painting subsided during the more restrictive political climate of the restoration of the 1850s. Nieuwerkerke and his colleagues were no doubt

Honoré Daumier, *Landscape painters. The first copies nature, the second copies the first.* Lithograph from *Le Charivari*, May 12, 1865.

> *"Beauty exists in nature and is encountered in the most varied of forms. As soon as one becomes aware of it, it belongs to art, or rather to the artist who is capable of recognizing it."*
>
> Gustave Courbet

thinking of painters such as those who gathered at Barbizon, a village in Fontainebleau Forest some forty miles (sixty kilometers) south of Paris, France. Since the 1830s, Barbizon had attracted those artists who wanted to turn from history to landscape painting. Unlike the Classicists, these artists did not paint the gently undulating Italian *campagna* at sunset, strewn with picturesque ruins. They painted the nature they beheld in front of them. They captured simple subjects in sketches or made studies of social milieux, a good example being Millet's depictions of peasant life (see ill. p.176).

As if their choice of subject matter was not revolutionary enough, these artists also worked outdoors. At the beginning of the century, English landscape painters had turned their backs on their French models and had moved their studios into the countryside. In England, where artistic life was dominated

not by an academy with an illustrious tradition but by private commissions, portraits and landscapes were highly regarded as the subjects of paintings. And now the Barbizon artists were also painting *en plein air* (in open air). Although mostly making sketches that they would later work on in the studio, some completed smaller canvases on the spot. Once oil paints began to be sold inexpensively in tin tubes around the middle of the century and paint dealers started to sell ready-primed canvases, painting outdoors became considerably easier. Even studies gradually acquired a new importance, not least for the collector, because they offered a more immediate impression of the natural scene than pictures worked on in the studio. What had previously ended up on the studio floor was now considered an artwork.

Nevertheless, landscape painters were criticized: "It is such a pity that this landscape painter [Daubigny] who possesses such authentic, correct, and natural feeling, is content to produce a mere impression and neglects details so. His pictures are only sketches and are poorly worked out. Objects are defined by apparent or real contours but Daubigny's landscapes display nothing more than patches of color lying next to each other" (Rewald).

To their opponents, the works of the Barbizon landscape painters lacked clear outlines and their details were not well enough delineated in terms of color—to say nothing of surface finish.

They were, nevertheless, represented in the Universal Exhibition of 1855. Jean-Baptiste-Camille Corot (1796–1875), the oldest member of the Barbizon circle, showed no fewer than

Gustave Courbet, *The Calm Sea*, 1869.
Oil on canvas, 23½ x 28¾ in. (60 x 73 cm).
The Metropolitan Museum of Art, New York, H.O. Havemeyer Collection.

▷ Jean-Baptiste-Camille Corot, *Early Morning Mist*, 1860.
Oil on canvas, 14¼ x 21¾ in. (36 x 55 cm).
Private collection.

six pictures (see ill. p.23). However, the numerous critics who attended the exhibition paid barely any attention to these works. Official honors were not in the offing for landscape painters widely associated with the republican ideas of the opposition. The laurels (in the form of the exhibition medals) were all won by history painters. In terms of sales, however, landscapes had the edge. The French bourgeoisie collected landscapes and the Barbizon School painters were represented by Parisian art dealers, so they were assured of good prices for their work. There were many artists dedicated to landscape painting during the Second Empire and they were able to show their work in the Salons. The recognition enjoyed by the painters of history paintings, which enjoyed a more prestigious reputation, was, however, denied them. Their image did not change for the better until 1871, under the Third Republic.

Artists, meanwhile, thought highly of Barbizon as a destination for open-air painting. In the early 1860s, the landscape painters who worked there were joined by a younger generation of artists. Claude Monet, Pierre-Auguste Renoir, Alfred Sisley, and Frédéric Bazille also found themselves working in the Fontainebleau region. They too became interested in the perception of light, color, and form in the open air, particularly with the forest as a motif (ill. p.24). Precisely because the genre was held in such low regard, these artists were able to try out new painting techniques and theories in their landscapes. But Barbizon gave the young painters more than just a new artistic stimulus.

The painters who gathered there formed a kind of artists' colony and worked in a loose community away from the rigid hierarchies that dominated the Parisian art world. Furthermore, although they had turned their backs on France's art capital, shown themselves to be critical of the Académie des Beaux-Arts, and chosen to devote themselves to landscape painting, the Paris scene was not uninterested in their work. Barbizon was close enough to the capital for these painters to be exhibited, discussed, and noted. This must have seemed an appealing prospect to all those artists looking for alternatives to the established art world.

Another such alternative was the free art school founded by Charles Suisse on the Île de la Cité in Paris in the 1820s. Students at the Académie Suisse received no tuition; they were simply provided with a model. Those who worked there included Pissarro, Monet, and later, Cézanne. Many future Impressionists also got to know each other at Charles Gleyre's studio (see ill. pp.26–7). Himself an academic painter who combined a Classical style with Asian elements, Gleyre traveled for some years in Italy, Greece, Egypt, Nubia, and Syria, before returning to Paris and establishing his studio. There he allowed his students abundant freedom, or as Pierre-Auguste Renoir put it, offered the advantage of "leaving them to their own devices." This latitude did not include landscapes and naturalistic depictions as worthy subjects for painting, but the master nevertheless succeeded in attracting Monet, Sisley, and Bazille to his studio, as well as Renoir, who worked there from 1861 to 1864.

THE FUTURE STARS:
MONET, SISLEY, BAZILLE, AND RENOIR

Claude Monet (ill. p.25) was born in Paris but grew up in Normandy, a region in northern France. His parents ran a grocery store in Le Havre. In the 1850s, while still a youth, he experienced a degree of success as a caricaturist. Having made the acquaintance of Eugène Boudin (1824–98) in Le Havre in 1856–57, he went on numerous painting trips with the landscapist over the next few years. Boudin's seascapes (ill. pp.28–9) only became accessible to the young Monet relatively late, but the established master was well aware of the debt he owed his teacher, declaring, "It is thanks to Eugène Boudin that I became a painter" (Arnold). The two artists stayed in touch for a long time, even after Monet moved to Paris to study in 1859. When Monet took up painting on the Normandy coast again after a year's military service in Algeria, he met the Dutch painter Johan Barthold Jongkind (1819–91). In addition to landscapes and seascapes, Jongkind also painted views of Paris. What interested him was the effect of different light conditions on his chosen subjects. Jongkind painted the cathedral of Notre Dame, Faubourg Saint-Jacques, and various other thoroughfares several times over in order to capture them at different times

Charles Gleyre, *Lost Illusions* or *Evening*, 1843.
Oil on canvas, 61¾ x 93¾ in. (157 x 238 cm).
Musée du Louvre, Paris.

PAGE 24
Pierre-Auguste Renoir, *Jules Le Cœur in the Forest of Fontainebleau*,
1866. Oil on canvas, 41¾ x 31½ in. (106 x 80 cm).
Museu de Arte, São Paulo, Brazil.

PAGE 25
Pierre-Auguste Renoir, *Portrait of Claude Monet*, 1875.
Oil on canvas, 33½ x 23¾ in. (85 x 60.5 cm).
Musée d'Orsay, Paris.

of day and year (ill. p.30). In Paris, Monet attended the
Académie Suisse, where he met Camille Pissarro and Charles
Gleyre's studio, where he befriended Frédéric Bazille and
Pierre-Auguste Renoir. Bazille helped to support Monet, who
was beset by frequent money worries. Because his family was
against his embarking on an artistic career, cash remittances
from home were the exception rather than the rule. The artist's
financial situation deteriorated even further, as did his general
relationship with his family, when around 1865 he formed a
liaison with seamstress Camille Doncieux, whom they deemed
to be his social inferior.

as art critic would later be of enormous importance to Impressionists. Mère Anthony is just visible in the background, while her daughter Nana can be seen clearing the table. In 1867, Renoir moved in with Bazille, who later shared his home with Sisley and Monet (ill. pp.60–61).

Alfred Sisley (ill. p.32) was born in Paris, though of English parents who had settled in France for professional reasons in 1839. He initially embarked on a commercial career, following in the footsteps of his parents. However, he started spending more and more time working at Charles Gleyre's studio, while benefiting from his father's support during the early stages of his artistic career. During the 1860s Sisley frequently worked alongside Monet, Renoir, and Bazille. When Gleyre's studio closed its doors in 1864, Sisley and his friends were drawn in the direction of Barbizon. Throughout his life, Sisley painted almost nothing but landscapes. After Barbizon his favorite open-air studio was the area between Bougival and Argenteuil, some twelve miles (twenty kilometers) west of Paris. He painted an avenue of chestnuts there several times over and his *Avenue of Chestnut Trees Near La Celle-Saint-Cloud* of 1867 was accepted for the Salon.

Frédéric Bazille (ill. p.33) came from Montpellier in southern France. His father was a Languedoc winegrower. In 1862, Bazille, Jr. left for Paris to attend medical college,

> *"Remember young man, when painting a figure, one should always recall the Ancients. Nature is very good as an aid to study, my young friend, but it holds no other interest. Style, you understand, is everything."*
>
> *Charles Gleyre to Claude Monet, 1862*

Pierre-Auguste Renoir, whose family had moved from Limoges to Paris in 1845, trained initially as a porcelain painter. He entered Gleyre's studio at the age of twenty and soon began going on expeditions with Monet, Sisley, and Bazille to the forests around Fontainebleau. In 1866, Renoir painted a group portrait of some of his fellow artists at "Mère Anthony's Inn," a popular artists' haunt in Marlotte (ill. p.31). Jules Le Cœur, who had settled in Marlotte to paint the year before, stands behind the Belgian painter Georges van den Bos. Opposite the Belgian sits Alfred Sisley with a copy of *L'Événement*. Émile Zola had recently been hired by the newspaper and his contributions

paid for by his father. Before long, however, he began to pursue artistic ambitions and started working in Gleyre's studio, where he met Monet, Renoir, and Sisley. Bazille became a close friend of Monet and was chosen as godfather to his son Jean in 1860. In 1864, Bazille gave up medicine and left with Monet to paint in Honfleur on the Normandy coast, where Boudin and Jongkind were working *en plein air*. Just two years later, Sisley, meanwhile, was able to tell his parents of his plans to exhibit at the Salon, where two of his works—landscapes painted near Fontainebleau—were ultimately accepted.

Eugène Boudin, *Beach Scene at Trouville*, 1871.
Oil on panel, 8½ x 15¾ in. (21.4 x 40.3 cm). Christie's, London.

Johan Barthold Jongkind, *Faubourg Saint-Jacques, Paris*, 1864.
Watercolor on paper, 13¼ x 17 in. (33.5 x 43 cm).
Musée Carnavalet, Paris.

Jongkind was born in The Netherlands in 1819 and trained at the
Academy of Drawing in The Hague before moving to Paris at the age of
twenty-six. He was guided toward a free and ever-simpler brushstroke
by his interest in the way atmospheric conditions affect a subject. This
caused Monet to admit freely that it was to the Dutchman, whom he met
in Le Havre in 1862, that he owed the "definitive education of my eye."

▷ Pierre-Auguste Renoir, *At the Inn of Mère Anthony*, 1866.
Oil on canvas, 76½ x 51½ in. (194 x 131 cm).
Nationalmuseum, Stockholm.

"*At the Inn of Mère Anthony* is a picture of which I retain extremely
pleasant memories. Not because I find it particularly exciting as a
painting but because it reminds me of the wonderful Mère Anthony
and her inn in Marlotte, the area's original watering hole. The subject
of the picture is the saloon, which also served as the dining room.
The old woman wearing the bonnet is Mère Anthony herself and the
magnificent young woman who serves the drinks is the waitress Nana.
The white dog, which had a wooden leg, was called Toto. I had a few
of my friends, including Sisley and Le Cœur, pose around the table.
As I show in my painting, the room was covered with pictures that
were painted directly onto the walls. They were unpretentious but
often very good, the work of regulars at the inn. The picture of Murger
[Henri Murger, 1822–61, a French writer] visible in the top left-hand
corner is by me."   Pierre-Auguste Renoir, 1918

Pierre-Auguste Renoir, *Portrait of Alfred Sisley*, 1876.
Oil on canvas, 26¼ x 21¼ in. (66.4 x 54.2 cm).
The Art Institute of Chicago, IL, U.S.

▷ Pierre-Auguste Renoir, *Frédéric Bazille at his Easel*, 1867.
Oil on canvas, 41¼ x 29 in. (105 x 73.5 cm).
Musée d'Orsay, Paris.

THE SALON

"Imagine the Salon as an enormous artistic ragout that is set before us each year. Every painter and every sculptor contributes an ingredient." By the time Émile Zola drew this comparison in his first piece of art criticism in 1866, the "ragout" was already a dish with a venerable tradition. Founded by Louis XIV in 1667, the Salon was initially the occasion on which works that originated in the Académie Royale de Peinture et de Sculpture were presented to the public.

Giuseppe Castiglione, *The Salon Carré in the Louvre*, 1861.
Oil on canvas, 27¼ x 40½ in. (69 x 103 cm). Musée du Louvre, Paris.

The academy and its exhibition, which was held every two years, had set the tone for the art scene in France since the seventeenth century. Before the French Revolution the Salon exhibitions mainly reflected the taste of the royal court. After 1789, artists who were not graduates of the Académie des Beaux-Arts, the institute that succeeded the Académie Royale de Peinture et de Sculpture, were also allowed to exhibit. The early exhibitions were held in the Salon Carré of the Louvre, still at that time a royal palace. The room also gave the exhibition its name, which was retained despite several changes of venue. Since 1857, the Salon was held in the Palais de l'Industrie on the Champs-Élysées (ill. pp.12–13).

Inclusion in the exhibition meant more than just a rung on the career ladder. For a long time, the Salon was the only platform on which artists could show their paintings or sculpture to a wider public—and this was therefore the best opportunity artists had to stimulate a demand for work that by this time was seldom produced on commission. After the revolution, any artist could apply to be included and the volume of submissions was correspondingly high. Female artists could also exhibit, although they only represented a small minority—a mere twelve percent or so of the total in 1869. The admission procedure, which has been researched in depth by Jane Mayo Roos, was extremely complex.

Several months before the Salon opened, the regulations, drawn up generally by the superintendent of fine arts, were published in the press. Who could deliver how many works and when? How would the jury be constituted? What competitions were being run and what medals were up for grabs?

In 1801, 268 artists presented 485 works. In 1848, the jury was abandoned and over 5,000 works were exhibited. The job of matching the number of works accepted for display with the amount of space available was eventually handed back to a jury drawn from members of the Académie des Beaux-Arts

making the rules and the Salon juries who selected or rejected the works of art grew louder and louder.

In view of the career-enhancing effect of the prizes and scholarships offered, participation in the Salon remained the most important factor in determining the market worth of an artist. Artists who wanted to find a buyer for their work in Paris, at that time the center of the art world, had no alternative but to exhibit at the Salon. The prosperous bourgeoisie liked to invest in art, but more importantly they liked to invest in art that came with the Salon "stamp of quality." Artists who were

Édouard Dantan, *A Corner of the 1880 Salon*, 1880.
Oil on canvas, 38¼ x 51¼ in. (97.2 x 130.2 cm).
Private collection.

Honoré Daumier, *Upon seeing one's own portrait hanging in the Salon*, no. 59 in the series *Les Beaux Jours de la Vie* from *Le Charivari*, 1845. Bibliothèque Nationale, Paris.

and thus the jurors for the 1859 Salon found only 3,045 of 8,000 works submitted worthy of display.

Zola took his comparison with the art of cookery even further. The Salon (in this case that of 1866) did not afford visitors an overview of French art, he claimed, precisely because responsibility lay mainly with the chefs "appointed especially to perform this delicate task" (in other words, the jury). The jury's decisions came in for strong criticism from those who found themselves rejected. The consequences of this criticism were twofold. First, the rules were changed; second, a Salon des Refusés was established in 1863. In order to prevent a further wave of protest, it was decided to hold the Salon annually instead of every two years. Only a quarter of the jury members would be appointed by the academy administration while the remainder would be made up of previous medal-winners. Although these changes looked like a liberalization, they altered very little as the rejected artists still had no right to play any part in the selection of the jury members. Criticism of those at the Académie des Beaux-Arts who were responsible for

rejected by the Salon or who were unable to establish any contact with persons of influence had subsequently to try to make a mark with large formats or sensational subject matter. Only those artists whose work stood out had any chance of finding potential buyers. The hordes of visitors to the exhibition—30,000 interested viewers could easily pass through on an admission-free Sunday—included not only wealthy collectors but also officials who were responsible for buying art for museums and other public buildings. This made the exhibition, which generally opened at the beginning of May and ran for several weeks, the indisputable high point of the Parisian art year. The Salon retained its monopoly over both taste and sales well into the second half of the nineteenth century. Even in 1881, the year the state handed responsibility for organizing the exhibition to an artists' association, Renoir described the importance of the art forum to the dealer Durand-Ruel as follows: "There are barely fifteen art lovers in the whole of Paris capable of recognizing a painter who is not represented in the Salon. And at least 80,000 who will buy any old canvas by an artist who is" (Rewald).

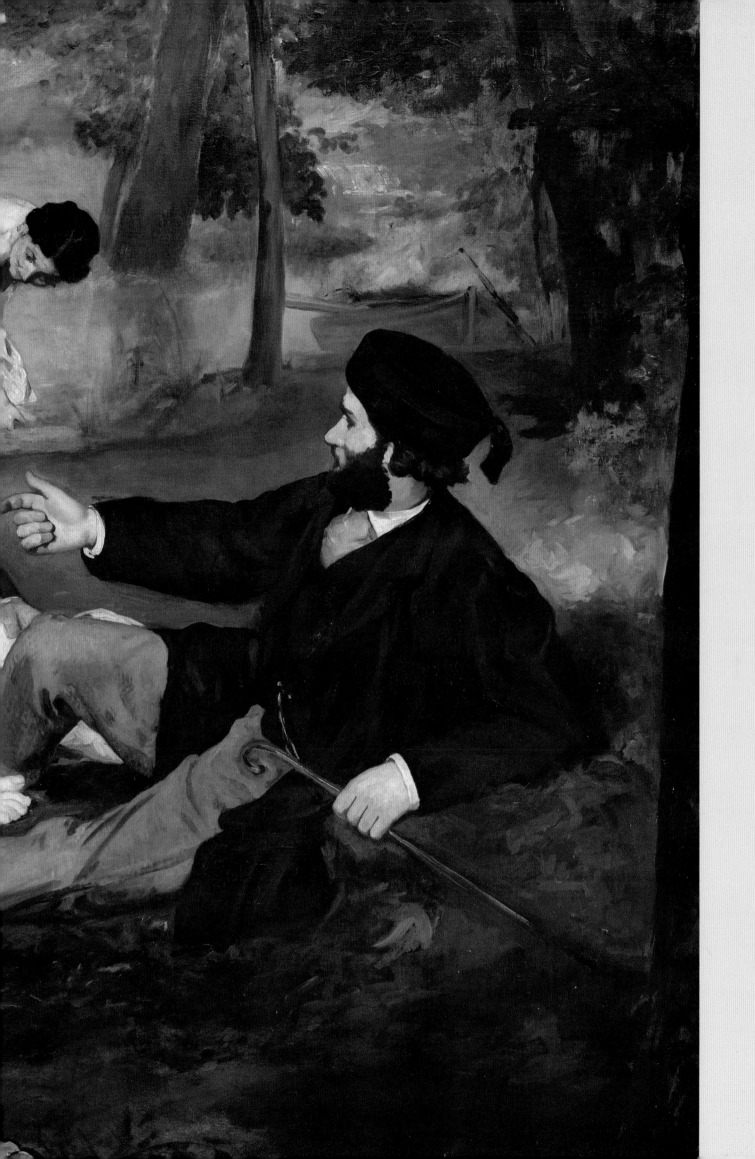

THE SALONS OF THE 1860S

Edgar Degas, *Portrait of Édouard Manet*, 1864.
Pencil on paper, approx. 23½ x 11¾ in. (60 x 30 cm). Private collection.

"Among those rejected this time were Édouard Manet and Ernest-Paul Brigot, who have had paintings accepted in previous years. Clearly they cannot have become significantly worse artists than they were before…. It seems logical to me that the pictures of a painter that are thought worthy of inclusion today should not simply be excluded tomorrow" (Zola). Writer and journalist Émile Zola, in whose first Salon report dated April 27, 1866, these critical lines were published, was not alone in his surprise. A large part of the Parisian art world was also wondering why Manet had been excluded from the Salon that year.

Just as changeable and inscrutable was the Salon policy of the early 1860s, as the example of Édouard Manet demonstrates. Rejected in 1860, the thirty-year-old painter (ill. p.38) from an upper middle-class background, who had spent six years in the studio of history painter Thomas Couture, became an unexpected success the following year. Although his work *The Spanish Singer* (ill. p.39) had been poorly hung, it was praised by Théophile Gautier and also made a good impression on Delacroix and Ingres. In the end, *The Spanish Singer* was moved to a better position and received an "honorable mention." Manet's enthusiasm for Spanish painting of the seventeenth and eighteenth centuries found expression in many of his early works. In the Louvre he studied the paintings of Velázquez, Zurbarán, and Goya. The influence of Goya's portraits can be seen, for example, in Manet's portrait of the Spanish dancer Lola Melea (ill. p.40), who performed in Paris with the Camprubí company of Madrid, Spain. Manet's penchant for Spanish themes reflected the French craze for all things Spanish that was initiated by Napoleon III's marriage to the Spanish countess Eugénie. The painter's 1862 portrait of the dancer in her richly colored costume could not be said to have met with the same enthusiasm, however, despite Melea being so in tune with the spirit of the times. "Art of this kind may be honestly intentioned," wrote one critic in the *Gazette des Beaux-Arts* (Rewald), "but it is unhealthy, and we cannot take it upon ourselves to plead for Manet before the Salon jury."

In 1863, the Salon jury promptly rejected all three works presented by Manet and indeed turned away three-fifths of the 5,000-plus works submitted to its scrutiny. Under pressure from the rejected artists, Napoleon III declared himself willing to provide them with their own exhibition, the so-called Salon des Refusés.

▷ **Édouard Manet**, *The Spanish Singer*, 1860.
Oil on canvas, 58 x 45 in. (147.3 x 114.3 cm). The Metropolitan Museum of Art, New York, Gift of William Church Osborn.

PAGES 36–7
Édouard Manet, *Le déjeuner sur l'herbe* (detail), 1863.
Oil on canvas, 82 x 104 in. (208 x 264 cm). Musée d'Orsay, Paris.

◁ **Édouard Manet**, *Lola de Valence*, 1862. Oil on canvas, 48½ x 36¼ in. (123 x 92 cm). Musée d'Orsay, Paris.

Édouard Manet, *Le déjeuner sur l'herbe*, 1863. Oil on canvas, 82 x 104 in. (208 x 264 cm). Musée d'Orsay, Paris.

But this measure merely presented artists with a different problem: "To exhibit means exposing oneself to public ridicule in the event of the picture ultimately being judged bad; this would be seen as proof of the jury's impartiality and justify the institution, not just today, but in the future too. Not to exhibit, on the other hand, means declaring oneself incapable of admitting one's shortcomings, which would also contribute to the glorification of the jury." Jules Castagnary's analysis of the situation hit the nail on the head. When the Salon des Refusés finally opened, visitors flocked to the exhibition. The reason was not so much to enjoy art as to laugh at it. And the selection committee had made it easy for them. Looking back, one English critic wrote of the jury's unerring talent for hanging the worst pictures in the best positions.

In 1863, Manet decided to show his *Le déjeuner sur l'herbe* (ill. p.41) at the Salon des Refusés. As in previous works, the painter made no secret of his love of the old masters in this picture: his inspiration came from Titian's *Concert champêtre* and an engraving by Marcantonio Raimondi of Raphael's *Judgment of Paris*. The picnic in a forest clearing is shared by two men and two women. The woman in the foreground is nude and, as a result, the painting caused an outrage. Criticism was provoked not only by the fact that a well-known prostitute, Victorine Meurent, had been the model for the naked figure but also by her posture. The nude figure was neither a legitimate element in a mythological scene (Alexandre Cabanel's painting *The Birth of Venus* won the gold medal at the Salon the same year despite presenting a far more wanton female nude), nor did she wear a devoted or modest expression; instead she fixes the viewer with a bold stare. So, instead of being able to enjoy the picture in secret, the viewer is implicated in the action in a highly indiscreet way. Manet was also strongly criticized for his treatment of perspective. However, very few critics attempted to shed light on his relationship with his artistic models.

To recap, whereas Manet had been honored in 1861 for his *Spanish Singer*, just two years later all the works he submitted were rejected. It was no surprise, then, that he started looking around for alternatives to the Salon. In 1863, he showed fourteen of his works at the gallery on Boulevard des Italiens of Louis Martinet, who had already exhibited many artists of the younger generation. Among these works was *Music in the Tuileries Gardens* (ill. pp.48–9), painted the previous year. In addition to himself (close to the left-hand edge), he also captured many other artists and friends in the picture, including poets Charles Baudelaire (an early admirer of his work) and Théophile Gautier, the painter Henri Fantin-Latour, the critic Zacharie Astruc, and the composer Jacques Offenbach. The concert is attended by neither antique heroes nor the gods of Mount Olympus, just friends, acquaintances, and companions. *Music in the Tuileries Gardens* is generally regarded, therefore, as Manet's response to Baudelaire's injunction to the artist to turn his attention to modern life. In his 1863 essay *The Painter of Modern Life*, Baudelaire called for rapidly executed pictures that would reflect the fast pace of modern life. Not only was Manet's subject matter innovative; so too was the technique he employed. Critics complained that the picture had been left unfinished in places, that Manet operated in a gray area between sketch and finished painting. They were confused by the flatness of the background and by the fact that Manet had loosely distributed distinct and indistinct elements without any apparent consideration to their distance from the viewer. They were also stumped by the short brushstrokes with which the faces of the two ladies in the foreground, for example, are depicted.

Manet was therefore very well accustomed to negative criticism by the following year when each of the two works he submitted was accepted for the Salon. Clearly all the negative discussion of *Le déjeuner sur l'herbe* at the Salon des Refusés had been forgotten. In 1864, he showed a religious painting and a bullfight. Another religious work was accepted by the jury the following year—along with *Olympia* (ill. pp.44–5), which caused another outrage. Olympia did not allow for unthinking, uninvolved enjoyment of the nude, any more than the prominent female figure in *Le déjeuner sur l'herbe* had done. Furthermore, the model for the picture (painted in 1863) had once again been Victorine.

◁ **Claude Monet**, *Le déjeuner sur l'herbe*, 1865.
Oil on canvas, 51¼ x 71¼ in. (130 x 181 cm). Pushkin Museum, Moscow.

PAGES 44–5
Édouard Manet, *Olympia*, 1863.
Oil on canvas, 51¼ x 74¾ in. (130.5 x 190 cm). Musée d'Orsay, Paris.

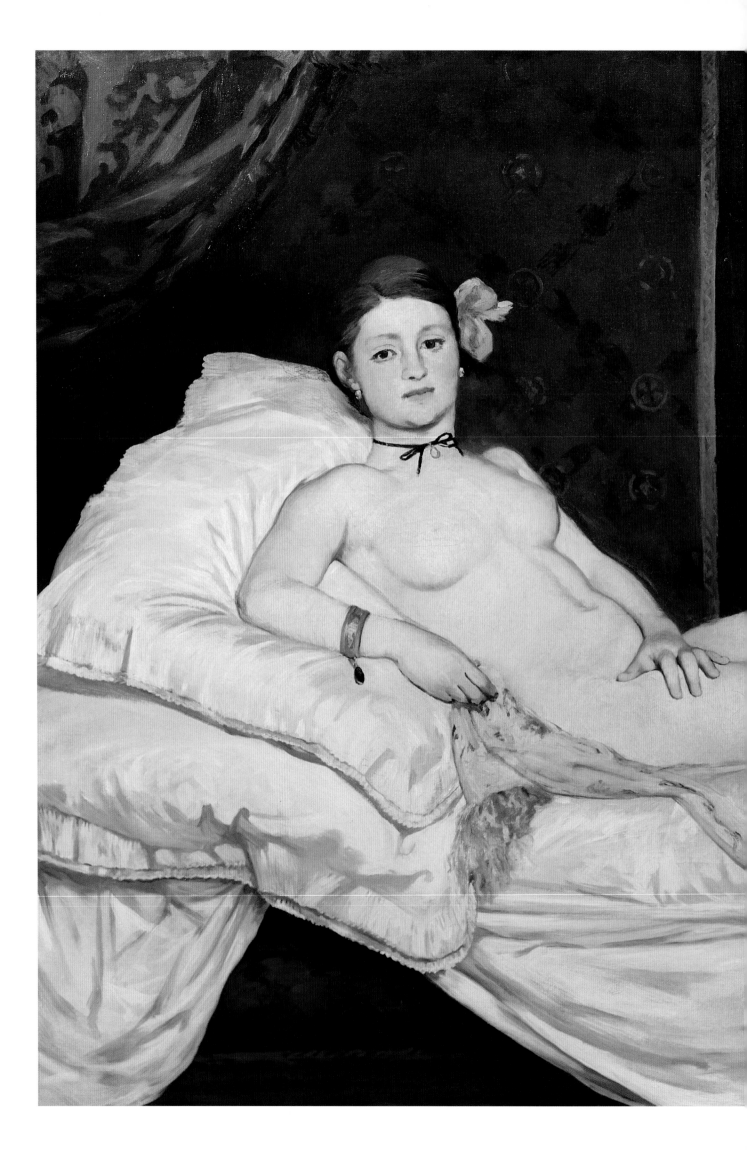

Camille Pissarro, *Pontoise*, ca. 1867. Oil on canvas, 32 x 39¼ in. (81 x 100 cm). Národní Galerie, Prague.

▷ **Édouard Manet**, *Berthe Morisot with a Bouquet of Violets*, 1872. Oil on canvas, 21¾ x 15¼ in. (55 x 39 cm). Musée d'Orsay, Paris.

Too ugly, far too apathetic, and insufficiently coquettish was the general verdict. Manet's inspiration, in particular a work by Titian, barely interested the critics, one of whom demanded flatly that *Olympia* be hung "high up, out of sight." Talk was of the "already somewhat decayed Olympia," of the "Odalisque with the yellow belly…this shameful model picked up who knows where" (Rewald).

Twenty-five years after its Salon debut, the picture that had caused such a furor was once again the center of attention. In 1890, Manet's widow wanted to sell the work and an American buyer was already interested. Claude Monet immediately set about trying to save *Olympia* for the nation. With the support of nearly one hundred colleagues, he succeeded in raising

PAGES 48–9
Édouard Manet, *Music in the Tuileries Gardens*, 1862.
Oil on canvas, 30 x 46½ in. (76.2 x 118.1 cm).
The National Gallery, London.

20,000 francs. The picture was duly acquired and donated to the Musée du Luxembourg in Paris.

ON THE PATH TO FAME: MONET, RENOIR, BAZILLE, PISSARRO, DEGAS, MORISOT, AND CÉZANNE

In 1866, Manet again submitted two works to the Salon. Neither his portrait of a boy musician, *The Fifer*, nor that of Philibert Rouvière in the role of Hamlet, *The Tragic Actor*, met with the jury's approval. Alongside Manet and hundreds of other artists trying to get accepted for the Salon that year were six men and one woman who were to become known over the course of the next decade as the "Impressionists": Monet, Renoir, Bazille, Pissarro, Degas, Morisot, and Cézanne.

Monet had made his first submissions to the Salon (two landscapes) the year before and both had been accepted. For

Edgar Degas, *The Bellelli Family*, 1858–67.
Oil on canvas, 78¾ x 98½ in. (200 x 250 cm). Musée d'Orsay, Paris.

▷ **Claude Monet**, *Camille* or *The Woman in the Green Dress*, 1866. Oil on canvas, 89¾ x 58¾ in. (228 x 149 cm). Kunsthalle Bremen, Germany.

the 1866 Salon he was planning his own version of *Le déjeuner sur l'herbe* in a work that combined landscape with figures and betrayed Manet's influence on the young painter. The model for the male figures in the twenty-foot (six-meter) wide canvas was Monet's friend and fellow artist Frédéric Bazille. The model for the female figures was his future wife Camille. However, Monet had misjudged the monumental dimensions of the picture. As the Salon drew near, the painter started to run out of time and money. The massive canvas had to be pawned and ultimately cut into sections. An impression of the compositional idea behind the painting is given by the smaller Moscow version of the same subject, which had probably been a study (ill. pp.42–3). Instead of *Le déjeuner sur l'herbe*, the painting Monet eventually submitted was *Camille*, otherwise known as *The Woman in the Green Dress* (ill. p.51). This rapidly painted, larger-than-life-size portrait presented a view of his beloved from the rear, showing

her face in profile—an unusual angle for a portrait. The picture caused a sensation and was admired by the critics Émile Zola and Jules Castagnary.

Renoir had submitted his first work to the Salon in 1863. It was rejected, but he chose not to exhibit it in the Salon des Refusés held that same year. The following year he was successful and was thus able to make his Salon debut. In 1865, his submissions were also accepted but in 1866, the jurors accepted only the smaller of the works he presented.

Frédéric Bazille tried for the Salon for the first time in 1866 with a still life and a figure painting. As he feared, the large-format figure painting was rejected and only the still life (with fish) was accepted. When viewing the work of unknown artists it was common Salon practice to accept small-format pictures and reject large-format works. This had been Renoir's experience too.

Camille Pissarro was born on the island of St. Thomas in the Antilles and arrived in Paris in 1855 at the age of twenty-five. There he attended the Académie Suisse.

Like Manet, but his junior by two years, Pissarro submitted work to the Salon for the first time in 1859. Unlike the Parisian painter, however, he was immediately accepted. There then followed a few Salons without success before two of his paintings were again accepted in 1864. Pissarro was also successful in 1865, when he found himself in the company of Monet, Renoir, Sisley, and Bazille (who were all painting in Barbizon at the time). His 1866 submissions, landscapes as in the previous years, were also admitted to the Parisian "temple of art" that was the Salon.

Edgar Degas, a Parisian, first exhibited at the Salon in 1865. The son of an aristocratic banker, he attended the École des Beaux-Arts briefly in 1855 but trained mostly by himself in the Louvre. Some five hundred drawings and paintings copied from old masters survive by him. Between 1854 and 1859, Degas lived mainly in Italy, where he developed an enthusiasm for the Renaissance masters. He returned to Paris in 1859 and met Manet in the Louvre three years later. Like Manet, Degas confined himself more or less to the figure and produced a number of history paintings before turning to modern subjects. During the 1860s he painted numerous portraits. Unlike many other painters, this was not out of necessity. *The Bellelli Family* (ill. p.50), the group portrait of the family of his aunt, Baroness Bellelli, was begun in Italy but not finished until 1867, when it was shown at the Salon. The work was hung in such a poor position, however, that it received hardly any attention, just like his previous year's submission, a painting of a horse race.

Berthe Morisot (ill. p.47) was accepted for the Salon on her first attempt. Born into a wealthy family in 1841, she was given drawing lessons as a young girl. In Paris this private tuition was continued by the painter Joseph Guichard, as women were still excluded not only from the École des Beaux-Arts, but from many private ateliers as well. Henri Fantin-Latour introduced Morisot to Manet in 1867 while they were working in the Louvre. Support for her work also came from Camille Corot, a family acquaintance, who likewise gave the young artist lessons.

The Provençal Paul Cézanne (ill. p.55) began submitting work to the Salon in 1863, having followed his childhood friend Émile Zola to Paris in 1861. As he had been turned down for the École des Beaux-Arts, he worked at Académie Suisse, where he met Bazille and Pissarro. After being turned down for the Salon yet again in 1866, he sent a letter of protest to the administrators in which he complained about the jury regulations and asked that another Salon des Refusés be held.

Claude Monet, *View of the Tuileries Gardens, Paris*, 1876.
Oil on canvas, 20¾ x 28¼ in. (53 x 72 cm). Musée Marmottan, Paris.

His first letter remained unanswered and so he wrote to the superintendent of fine arts again on April 19, 1866, "I simply want to say to you again that I am unable to recognize the unfair judgment of your colleagues, whom I did not personally authorize to judge me. I write to you again in order to emphasize my demand. I wish to present myself to the public and exhibit my pictures despite everything. This wish does not appear to me to be excessive. Were you to ask every artist in my position, you would receive the same answer from all without exception: that they reject the jury and would like to participate in an exhibition that should self-evidently be open to any serious artist. The Salon des Refusés should therefore be reintroduced. Even if I am there alone, it is my most ardent desire to show everyone that I care as little to be confused with the gentlemen of the jury as they appear to care to be confused with me" (Rewald).

SALON POLICY AND THE "REFUSÉS"

While all the artists mentioned above, whether accepted or rejected by the Salon, were just starting out on their careers, Gustave Courbet had been appearing regularly before the Salon jury for many years and, moreover, was regarded as a capable businessman—the archetype of the provincial who makes it in the capital. He had been submitting work to the exhibition since 1841—albeit with a few rejections, on which occasions he had made his opinions heard loud and clear. Because of the numerous medals he had won, the painter had been exempted from having to submit his works to the jury. In 1866, however, he got into a dispute with the superintendent of fine arts over the purchase of his painting *Woman with a Parrot*. Nieuwerkerke maintained that agreement had never been reached over the sale of the painting. Courbet was of a different opinion. A heated disagreement ensued that remained unresolved, and despite all his honors, Courbet became persona non grata.

That some of the young painters had been admitted to the Salon of 1866 and some had not was less of a talking point than Courbet's and Manet's wrangles with the Beaux-Arts administration. In April 1866, there were protests against the acceptance procedure after Manet's rejection had been reported in the newspapers. The reason his anything other than provocative paintings had not been accepted that year remained unclear. Some critics saw his rejection as a late response to the previous year's *Olympia* scandal. Yet another event occurred in 1866 that drew public attention to the decisions of the Salon jury: The painter Jules Holtzapffel committed suicide after his work had been refused. This incident was hotly debated in the press—nowhere more so than in *L'Événement*, which

Camille Pissarro and Paul Cézanne, ca. 1873.
Photograph. Private collection.

◁ **Édouard Manet**, *Portrait of Émile Zola*, 1868.
Oil on canvas, 57¾ x 45 in. (146.5 x 114 cm). Musée d'Orsay, Paris.

on April 30, published one of Émile Zola's most controversial articles. Although the jurors' decision was not held to be the sole reason for the painter's death, the jury had forfeited even more sympathy than in previous years.

For the time being there were no repercussions to the protests from artists and critics. In the 1867 Salon, Degas showed two family portraits, and Morisot a landscape. The submissions of Pissarro, Cézanne, and Sisley were rejected as were large-format pictures by Monet, Bazille, and Renoir. In Monet's case in particular, the jury's decision caused astonishment after his *Camille* had been accepted and well received the previous year. Following the announcement of who had been accepted and who had been rejected, over one hundred artists sent a letter to Nieuwerkerke demanding that another Salon des Refusés be held.

The letter was written by Frédéric Bazille and below his signature, Sisley, Guillemet, and Manet added theirs. A number of artists who had been admitted to the official Salon, such as Jongkind and Daubigny, also signed. Their signatures were enclosed on a second sheet. When nothing happened,

A crane being used to unload exhibition materials for the Paris Universal Exhibition of 1867. Contemporary wood engraving based on a drawing by Fellmann.

▷ **Édouard Manet**, *The Exposition Universelle in Paris*, 1867. Oil on canvas, 42½ x 77¼ in. (108 x 196 cm). Nasjonalgalleriet, Oslo.

twenty-five artists, again including Renoir, Monet, Pissarro, and Bazille, sent another letter to the Salon administration in mid-April. When it became clear that this second letter had also failed to produce a satisfactory result, the painters started looking around for other ways. They had been impressed by the independent events organized by Courbet and Manet, who had opened up his studio to the public after being rejected in 1866. Manet, Monet, and others also occasionally displayed their work in art dealers' windows. This was not a viable alternative to the Salon, however, as it meant submitting to the judgment of the individual dealer in question. New ideas began to circulate. In spring 1867, Bazille, one of the organizers of the petition to Nieuwerkerke, wrote to his parents, "I'm not sending anything else to the jury. It's just too ridiculous…to be exposed to their whims…. This view is shared by a dozen or so gifted young people. We've therefore decided to rent a large studio each year in which we can show however many pieces we wish" (Rewald). However, the artists were forced to abandon their plan in May as they were unable to raise the required sum of money.

Compared to the previous year, the 1867 Salon was poorly attended. For the same money the public found the Universal Exhibition on the opposite bank of the Seine a more appealing prospect. For a whole seven months, novelties from all over the world beckoned on the Champ de Mars. Painting and sculpture, meanwhile, were allocated less space than in 1855.

Manet captured the 1867 exhibition site and its unique urban landscape (ill. pp.56–7) on canvas. From a high vantage point close to the Trocadéro, which was one of the most popular viewing points, the eye is drawn down to the Champ de Mars. It is almost impossible to make out the actual exhibition buildings or the Seine, which ought to appear in the middle distance. By simply not depicting the middle ground, Manet also solved the problem of perspective in an original way. His figures in the foreground give way directly to the panoramic landscape of the background.

The art historian Patricia Mainardi also discovered a kind of panorama in the foreground of the picture. The whole of society is represented here, from sightseers to soldiers; from workers to the wealthy. The picture was bold in terms of its execution; individual brushstrokes can be made out, even in the depiction of the figures. Overpainting along the left edge and the lack of a signature suggest that the painting may not have been finished. What is certain, however, is that the city

view remained in Manet's studio to the end of the painter's life and was never exhibited.

The artist's viewpoint may have been influenced in part by the difference of opinion over his participation in the Universal Exhibition. Manet had proposed a list of no fewer than thirty-five works that he wanted to exhibit on the Champ de Mars in 1867. Although the jury had not limited the number of submissions per artist, thirty-five could perhaps be seen as pushing the limit. Six of the pictures he proposed had already been rejected by another jury (the Salon), two of them the previous year. This would seem to indicate that Manet

was being deliberately provocative. His list of pictures was promptly rejected by the Universal Exhibition and the artist refused to resubmit individual works or even participate in the Salon. Instead he set about organizing his own exhibition—close to Courbet's, the older painter having decided once again to exhibit independently. Manet opened his exhibition of some fifty works at the end of May. The foreword in his specially printed catalog was written by Émile Zola and constituted a vehement defense of the artist.

Several months after the exhibition, Manet painted the writer's portrait (ill. p.54) and Zola in turn recorded how long and strenuous the sittings had been. Nothing is left to chance in this picture. The sitter's personality—or at least Zola the critic, the side of him that was so important to Manet—is reflected in his surroundings. On the wall above the desk hang a Japanese print, a reproduction of *Bacchus* by Velázquez, and in front of it, a copy of Manet's *Olympia*, which had caused such a scandal. Tucked behind the inkwell is a document on which the title "Manet" can be made out—it is the study in which Zola highlights the originality of Manet's work.

During the year after the Universal Exhibition, Manet's fortunes looked up. His portrait of Zola was accepted for the 1868 Salon, as was his second piece, *Young Lady in 1866 (Woman with a Parrot)*. A number of young artists benefited that year from the presence of landscape painter Charles Daubigny on the jury. Both of Pissarro's landscapes were accepted, although Zola noted in his review that they were both hung so high that visitors could barely see them. Of Monet's two views of the

> *"The artists I have been talking about have been called 'Impressionists' because most of them are striving visibly to convey a true-to-life impression of things and people.... But fortunately they all have their own individual style, their own unique way of seeing reality."*
>
> *Émile Zola*

coast near Le Havre, only one made it to the Salon but created a big impression. Bazille and Renoir even managed to exhibit large figure paintings, albeit in the *dépotoir*, the back room of the exhibition. Morisot and Degas were also represented. The only one to be rejected outright was, once again, Paul Cézanne. Overall, there were more works on display by the future Impressionists at the 1868 Salon than ever before. Nevertheless, this success was due to a change in the way the jury was elected rather than any permanent liberalization on the part of the organizers.

ÉMILE ZOLA AND THE "ACTUALISTS"

Émile Zola was the first person to define the Impressionist painters Monet, Bazille, and Renoir as a distinct group, labeling them the "Actualists" because of the modern subject matter of their pictures. In 1866, he began publishing a series of provocative Salon critiques in the Paris newspaper *L'Événement*.

These articles opened with an examination of the jury system and culminated in a demand for another Salon des Refusés (see pp.38 and 41). In 1868, Zola was again among the numerous critics of the official art policy who made their opinions known. Censorship of the press had been relaxed because of the second Paris Universal Exhibition. The critic Edmond About, for one, let off steam in the *Revue des Deux Mondes*, noting that the Salon space in the Palais de l'Industrie was neither a hothouse nor a hall but was used for both, and that the exhibited works included, appropriately enough, both art and vegetables. He mentioned the fact that a multiplicity of events of other kinds were being held in the Palais de l'Industrie alongside the art exhibition. Zola and others accused the organizers of the 1868 Salon of lacking a clear plan. Zola devoted his entire review to the new generation of painters. Unlike his reviews of previous Salons, he ignored the usual suspects completely, dismissing the entire establishment as contributing "a collection of mediocre works ranging from sentimental stupidity to the ludicrously serious" (Zola). Zola discussed the "Naturalists" Manet and Pissarro in some depth and followed this up with an article on the "Actualists" Monet, Bazille, and Renoir and another in which he turned his attention to Jongkind, Corot, and the sisters Berthe and Edma Morisot. Zola's articles were of enormous importance to the future Impressionists. He was, after all, the first critic to attempt to describe their artistic similarities.

The following year, not only were Zola's Actualists rejected, of a total 6,304 submitted works, only 4,230 were shown. Although two-thirds of that year's jury were elected by the entirety of painters who had previously exhibited in the Salon, most of the jurors—again with the exception of Daubigny—belonged to the conservative camp. The 2,000 rejected works included paintings by Monet that the artist promptly displayed in the window of an art dealer in Rue Latouche. Of Bazille's two pictures, one was accepted. Renoir and Pissarro also showed one small-format painting each. Berthe Morisot, who did not take part in the 1869 Salon, described Bazille's *View of the Village, Castelnau* (ill. p.59) in a letter to her sister Edma dated May 1, 1869, "Bazille has done something I like greatly: A young girl wearing a light-colored dress sits in the shade of a tree. Behind, in the distance, a village can be seen. The picture is full of light and sunshine. What he has attempted to do is what we have so often tried to do, depict a figure in the open air. And it seems to me that he has succeeded" (Rewald).

Bazille also seemed happy with his picture—which can be seen standing on the easel in *Bazille's Studio, 9 Rue de la Condamine* (ill. pp.60–61), painted the following year.

In 1869, Edgar Degas showed a portrait at the Salon; his second work was rejected. Cézanne was unsuccessful yet again.

Frédéric Bazille, *View of the Village, Castelnau*, 1868.
Oil on canvas, 51¼ x 35 in. (130 x 89 cm).
Musée Fabre, Montpellier, France.

F. Bazille 1868

Frédéric Bazille, *Bazille's Studio, 9 Rue de la Condamine*, 1870. Oil on canvas, 38½ x 50½ in. (98 x 128 cm). Musée d'Orsay, Paris.

Bazille's studio was the meeting place of the group of artists who became known as the Impressionists. On the easel is his painting *View of the Village, Castelnau* (ill. p.59), which he is showing to Monet and Manet. On the left of the picture, Zola is talking to Renoir (on the staircase) and the musician and critic Edmond Maître sits at the piano.

Édouard Manet, *The Execution of the Emperor Maximilian of Mexico*, 1868–69.
Oil on canvas, 99¼ x 120 in. (252 x 305 cm). Kunsthalle, Mannheim, Germany.

Édouard Manet, *Luncheon in the Studio*, 1868.
Oil on canvas, 46½ x 60½ in. (118.3 x 154 cm).
Bayerische Staatsgemäldesammlungen,
Neue Pinakothek, Munich, Germany.

Given the rather subsidiary role played by the
meal of the title, it would perhaps be more
accurate to regard Manet's painting as a portrait.
The name of the young dandy gazing past the
viewer from his position in the foreground is Léon
Koëlla Leenhoff (believed to be Manet's son). The
work failed to meet with any great enthusiasm at
the 1869 Salon but several decades later, Henri
Matisse was enchanted by Léon's black velvet
jacket, which he declared had been created out
of "pure black and light."

▷ Édouard Manet, *The Balcony*, 1868.
Oil on canvas, 67 x 49 in. (170 x 124.5 cm).
Musée d'Orsay, Paris.

Manet had decided not to submit his political picture *The Execution of the Emperor Maximilian* (ill. p.62), fearing censorship. Instead he presented *Luncheon in the Studio* (ill. p.62). Léon Koëlla Leenhoff, whose mother, Suzanne, Manet had married in 1863, leans against a table in the foreground, gazing outwards. Auguste Rousellin, a former pupil of Thomas Couture and a frequent guest in Manet's house, can be seen on the right of the picture, smoking, while a cat grooms itself next to a large curved sword and helmet. The maid in the background holds a coffee pot; a large pot plant looms over her. Critics thought the subject of the work too mundane and complained that there was no connection between the figures. The flat picture space and bold foreshortening met with little enthusiasm. Morisot reported, "Poor Manet is sad because as always the pictures he's showing are little appreciated by the public; he never fails to be surprised by it though" (Rewald). She went on to describe how she was afraid to see his second picture, for which she had been one of the models. Although it was an outdoor scene, *The Balcony* (ill. p.63) had been painted in the studio. Manet's other female model for the painting had been the cellist Fanny Claus.

His friend, the landscape painter Antoine Guillemet, was the model for the waiter who can barely be seen in the darkened room that forms the background to the balcony.

Unlike Manet, Claude Monet was concentrating on landscapes and seascapes during these years. He was drawn to the countryside around Paris and in Normandy (ill. pp.64–5). In 1867, he was staying in his father's house in Sainte-Adresse near Le Havre, France, where he painted *The Garden at Sainte-Adresse* (ill. pp.66–7). In this painting the terrace and sea account for nearly half the picture space. The flatness of the picture is underlined by the raised viewpoint and the emphasis on the horizontal. Terrace, water, and horizon seem to lie less behind one another than one above the other. The two-dimensional style is broken up mainly by the two flagpoles, which indicate spatial depth.

Monet referred to this picture as his "Chinese painting with flags." The compositional model actually originated in Japan—more specifically with a print in the series *Thirty-Six Views of Mount Fuji* created by Japanese artist Hokusai between 1829 and 1833. The woodcut entitled *On a Temple Balcony. The*

◁ **Claude Monet**, *The Beach at Sainte-Adresse*, 1867. Oil on canvas, 29¾ x 40¼ in. (75.8 x 102.5 cm). The Art Institute of Chicago, IL, U.S. Mr. and Mrs. Lewis Larned Coburn Memorial Collection.

Claude Monet, *On the Beach Promenade at Trouville*, 1870. Oil on canvas, 19¾ x 27½ in. (50 x 70 cm). Private collection.

Sazai Hall of the Temple of the 500 Rakan (ill. p.68) is defined by horizontals. The pictorial elements are set on the surface of the picture with no perspectival focal point. Fuji, the mountain sacred to the Japanese, recedes into the background.

Countless artists developed an enthusiasm for works like these, far removed from the traditions of European academic painting, during the second half of the nineteenth century. For well over two centuries, the Tokugawa shogunate had ruled in Japan, pursuing a policy of virtual isolationism in relation to foreign trade. However, U.S. Navy Commodore Matthew Perry had, in 1854, signed the Convention of Kanagawa with Japan, which began the process of the opening up of trade routes between Japan and the West. Prints by Japanese artists started to arrive in Europe in the middle of the nineteenth century as packing paper for imported Japanese goods. Hokusai's woodcut *The Great Wave of Kanagawa* (ill. p.68), became the best-known work of Japanese art in Europe. The first shop to sell Asian goods opened in Paris as early as 1862 and the display of Japanese prints and

craft products at the Universal Exhibition of 1867 started a craze for all things Asian. On the one hand, woodcuts, illustrated books, and painted surfaces appeared as subjects in European art; on the other, numerous artists were influenced by the compositional differences between Japanese and European art. In his choice of unusual perspectives, Degas showed that he too was familiar with the compositional principles of Japanese color woodblock prints. He often depicted his subjects from extreme angles above or below, left the center of a picture empty, or cut off figures at the edges (ill. p.157). Vincent van Gogh even entertained the idea of dealing in Japanese prints for a while. In 1878, the critic Théodore Duret described the influence of Japanese art on the Impressionists as follows: "When they first set eyes on Japanese pictures, in which the loudest colors are placed next to each other, the realization suddenly dawned that there were new ways of representing natural phenomena that had it not hitherto been considered possible to depict" (Smith).

Claude Monet, *The Garden at Sainte-Adresse*, 1867.
Oil on canvas, 38½ x 51¼ in. (98.1 x 129.9 cm).
The Metropolitan Museum of Art Purchase, New
York, Special contributions and funds given or
bequeathed by friends of the Museum, 1967.

Monet spent the summer of 1867 in Sainte-Adresse,
France, with his family, who are shown in this
painting. His cousin, Jeanne-Marguerite Lecadre,
stands with an unknown gentleman at the edge
of the terrace while his parents, seated in the
foreground, look out to sea.

Katsushika Hokusai, *On a Temple Balcony. The Sazai Hall of the Temple of the 500 Rakan*, from the series *Thirty-Six Views of Mount Fuji*, 1829–33. Color woodblock print, 9½ x 13½ in. (23.9 x 34.3 cm). British Museum, London.

▷ **Claude Monet**, *La Japonaise (Camille Monet in Japanese Costume)*, 1876. Oil on canvas, 91 x 40¼ in. (231 x 102 cm). Museum of Fine Arts, Boston, MA, U.S., 1951 Purchase Fund.

Katsushika Hokusai, *The Great Wave of Kanagawa*, from the series *Thirty-Six Views of Mount Fuji*, 1829–33. Color woodblock print, 9¾ x 14¼ in. (24.6 x 36.2 cm). Private collection.

◁ Vincent van Gogh, *Le Père Tanguy*, 1887–88.
Oil on canvas, 36¼ x 29½ in. (92 x 75 cm). Musée Rodin, Paris.

Pierre-Auguste Renoir, *La Grenouillère*, 1869. Oil on canvas,
25½ x 36¼ in. (65.1 x 92.1 cm). Kunstmuseum, Winterthur, Switzerland.

INNOVATIONS

In *The Garden at Sainte-Adresse*, Monet had shown how flowers and the surface of the water could be rendered with individual spots of color and short brushstrokes. This new development in his painting technique can be seen even more clearly in the paintings he produced two years later. In 1869, Monet and Renoir spent a lot of time working in the area around Paris. In the 1850s, the countryside surrounding the capital had started to become increasingly popular with day trippers, thanks to the arrival of the railroad connecting the capital with numerous places along the banks of the River Seine: Argenteuil, Bougival, Asnières. Renoir spent the summer of 1869 at his parents' house not far from Bougival. Monet ended up in the same area some twelve miles (twenty kilometers) west of Paris and that fall settled with his family in the village of Saint-Michel between Louveciennes and Bougival. The two painters often set up their easels alongside one another. They were both enchanted by the scenes they witnessed on the banks of the Seine. At one spot by a tributary of the Seine, called La Grenouillère ("frog pool"), was a restaurant and bathing pool that was popular with vacationers and artists alike. Swimmers would enter the water from a platform in the river known as a *camembert*. In Renoir's painting this little bathing island can be seen to the right of the picture (ill. p.71). Monet directs his gaze more toward the bank and jetty and uses cooler tones (ill. pp.72–3). The two pictures display clear differences in handling. More detail can be made out in Renoir's painting, whereas Monet uses shorter brushstrokes and renders the boats in the shady foreground of his picture with large patches of dark color. He depicts the group of bathers in the sun-dappled water behind the jetty with just a few dabs of paint and uses a variety of broad brushstrokes to capture the moving surface of the water in the foreground. The background colors, meanwhile, are lighter: white, light blue, pink, and lime green are used alongside one another. The leaves, particularly those in the top right corner of the picture, are merely sketched.

A brief glance back at Bazille's *View of the Village, Castelnau* (ill. p.59) underlines Monet's innovations: The reproduction of objects and their local color have become less important.

Each object in the picture, and the surface of the water in particular, is made up of its local color and the colors that surround it. Monet's free handling suggests that the work was only a sketch. In September 1869, the artist wrote of his progress, "I have been dreaming of a picture of bathers in La Grenouillère and have already made a few poor sketches but it remains a dream" (*Landschaft im Licht*). Nevertheless, the painter considered works like these to be altogether worthy of sale—especially because people were willing to buy. Monet also explained in a letter to Bazille that he preferred his studies to his studio paintings. Not so the Salon jurors, who refused both of his submissions for the 1870 Salon.

They did, however, find 5,434 other pieces of work worthy of display, thereby reflecting a general trend toward liberalization. The era of Superintendent Nieuwerkerke had come to an end and the Salon was opening up, as the large number of works exhibited in the Palais de l'Industrie demonstrated. Degas showed two portraits at the 1870 Salon and two of Manet's works were accepted. Renoir exhibited two figure paintings including his *Bather with Griffon* (ill. p.76), Pissarro showed two landscapes, Sisley two Parisian scenes, and Berthe Morisot two figure paintings: a portrait of her sister Edma and another of her mother and sister (ill. p.77). Cézanne's submissions were both rejected yet again. Frédéric Bazille, for one, was extremely pleased with the Salon: "I'm very happy. My picture has been hung well. Everybody notices it and talks about it. A lot of people find in it more to criticize than to praise but it has launched me and anything I now exhibit will be noticed" (Rewald).

Bazille was also "launched" on canvas at the same Salon—as one of the artists in Henri Fantin-Latour's group portrait. After spending a short time at the École des Beaux-Arts, Fantin-Latour (1836–1904) worked mainly in the Louvre. In 1867, he showed a portrait of Manet at the Salon and depicted the painter again three years later in *A Studio in Batignolles* (ill. pp.74–5). At this time Batignolles was still a rural district in northwest Paris between the Boulevard de Clichy and Montmartre. Manet, Renoir, Monet, and Bazille had all taken studios there and also appear in Fantin-Latour's group portrait. Manet is seated at the center of the picture in the process of painting artist and critic Zacharie Astruc, who had introduced Manet to Monet. Bazille is the tall figure standing with his hands clasped behind his back to the right of the picture. Monet can be made out behind him. Renoir and the German painter, Otto Scholderer, are standing behind Manet while Émile Zola (with outstretched hand) and the musician and critic, Edmond Maître, are standing behind Astruc. Critics referred to this group of artists as the "school of Batignolles" or—as Manet was the senior figure among them—"Manet's gang." Today they are better known as the "Impressionists."

Claude Monet, *Bathers at La Grenouillère*, 1869.
Oil on canvas, 28¾ x 36¼ in. (73 x 92 cm). The National Gallery, London.

Henri Fantin-Latour,
A Studio in Batignolles, 1870.
Oil on canvas,
80¼ x 107¾ in. (204 x 273.5 cm).
Musée d'Orsay, Paris.

◁ Pierre-Auguste Renoir, *Bather with Griffon*, 1870. Oil on canvas, 72½ x 45¼ in. (184 x 115 cm). Museu de Arte, São Paulo, Brazil.

Berthe Morisot, *Mother and Sister Reading*, 1869–70. Oil on canvas, 39¾ x 32¼ in. (101 x 81.8 cm). National Gallery of Art, Washington, DC.

LIGHT AND COLOR IN SCIENCE

In *Fishing Nets at Pourville* (ill. p.78), which Monet painted in 1882, the fishing nets of the title rise up vertically out of the water. The painter traveled to the Normandy coast a number of times that year. He painted the surface of the sea in all its myriad manifestations from calm and sunlit to storm-tossed, by no means confining himself to shades of blue. Under a warmly glowing evening sky, the sea in this painting shimmers with every conceivable color and also reflects the surrounding colors. To reproduce the effect of the light in paint, Monet uses short, curved brushstrokes side by side.

Claude Monet, *Fishing Nets at Pourville*, 1882.
Oil on canvas, 23½ x 32 in. (60 x 81 cm).
Haags Gemeentemuseum, The Hague, The Netherlands.

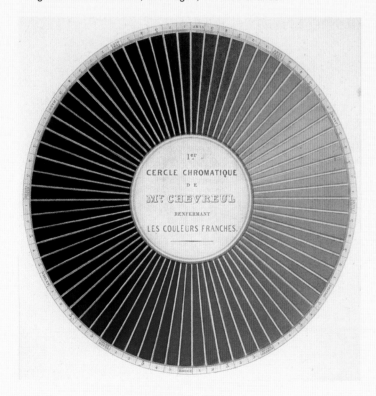

René Digeon, Color wheel of pure shades, 1864.
Steel engraving and color print.

In his handling of color, Monet had recourse to the scientific knowledge of the day, which held that outdoors, in nature, what people perceived were not so much concrete, objective colors as mixed colors that were formed into surfaces and objects by the eye. Monet advised the American painter Lilla Cabot Perry, who settled in Giverny, northern France, in 1889, to paint not objects and events but areas of color: "When you go out to paint, try to forget what object you have in front of your eyes, whether it's a tree, a house, a field, or whatever else. Think only: here's a small square of blue, there's a pink rectangle, there's a strip of yellow, and paint the shape and color exactly as you experience it until you have reproduced your innocent impression of the scene" (Smith).

The scientific implications of color theory and the theory of perception had a major impact on open-air painting and the rendering of light and color. Nineteenth-century painters were influenced in particular by the works of French chemist Eugène Chevreul. In his treatises, *The Law of Simultaneous Contrast of Colors* (1839) and *The Principles of Harmony and Contrast of Colours and their Applications to the Arts* (1864), Chevreul studies the composition of light and color (ill. p.166). He examines whether adjacent colors on the color wheel influence each other, and if so, how. He ascertains that colors located opposite one another on the color wheel create the strongest contrasts. These complementary contrasts are created by red and green, blue and orange, and yellow and violet. Chevreul and other researchers, such as the German physicist Hermann von Helmholtz, also looked into the effects of simultaneous contrast whereby in bright light the eye detects two shades in a particular color: its own and that opposite it on the color wheel. With his theory of "unconscious inference," Helmholtz also justified his view that the manner in which objects are visually perceived is influenced by perceptive mechanisms over which the human mind has no control.

These latest insights provided by the science of optics and the psychology of perception were widely discussed in artistic circles. Delacroix had already studied Chevreul's discoveries concerning contrasting complementaries and the Impressionists showed a particular interest in the rendering of shadows. They moved away from the notion that an object's shadow was darkness or an absence of color and could be expressed by making its local color darker. Instead they depicted areas of shadow using mainly complementary colors, as Sisley's *River Steamer and Bridge* (ill. p.79) demonstrates.

In 1887, Pissarro stressed to his son the importance to the Impressionists of scientific research into visual phenomena and the mechanics of sight: "De Bellio…would have me believe that investigations into the physics of light and color are of as little use to the artist as anatomy or the laws of optics. Dear God! If we hadn't known, thanks to the research of Chevreul and other scientists, how colors behave, we would never have been able to conduct our study of light with such confidence. I would not be able to differentiate between local color and illumination had science not discovered it. The same goes for complementary colors, contrasting colors, etc." (Smith). Of the Impressionists, it was Pissarro who took the greatest interest in the techniques employed by Georges Seurat. Seurat had conducted an in-depth investigation into the perception of color and in the mid-1880s started to paint pictures made up out of countless tiny dots of primary colors and their complementaries. Even the shadows under the bridge leading toward the Eiffel Tower in his 1889 painting (ill. p.79) are, upon closer inspection, brightly painted, comprising dots of bright blue, orange, and yellow, shades of green, violet, and pink, and so on. In Seurat's pictures, mixing the colors is not the task of the painter, it is the task of the viewer's eye. As Seurat knew from contemporary research into the subject, the human brain is capable of recognizing objects in the multiplicity of colored dots. The Neo-Impressionists centered around Seurat gave their use of color a scientific basis, though their rigid technique ruled out any development. Whereas Signac put this theory into words eight years after Seurat's death with his manifesto *From Eugène Delacroix to Neo-Impressionism* (1899), the Impressionists for their part did not develop a color theory of their own and left very few written descriptions of their techniques. Renoir, the Impressionist's most important colorist, summed up his working method as follows: "I want my red to ring out like a bell. If I'm unsuccessful at first, I add more red and other colors, too, until I achieve the right sound…. I follow neither rules nor a specific method" (Welton).

Alfred Sisley, *River Steamer and Bridge*, 1871. Oil on canvas, 18 x 24 in. (46 x 61 cm). Collection of Akram Ojjeh, Neuilly, France.

Georges Seurat, *The Eiffel Tower*, ca. 1889. Oil on canvas, 9½ x 6 in. (24.1 x 15.2 cm). Fine Arts Museum of San Francisco, CA, U.S.

THE IMPRESSIONISTS REQUEST THE PLEASURE:
A SPACE FOR NEW SUBJECTS

Cham, real name Amédée Charles Henri de Noé, cartoon satirizing the first Impressionist exhibition, Paris. Bibliothèque Nationale, Paris.

In his essay *The Painter of Modern Life*, published in 1863, Charles Baudelaire offered the following definition of modernity: "Modernity is the transitory, the fleeting, the random, it is one half of art, whose other half is the eternal and immutable." It was to this first half, the manifestations and conditions of modern life, that artists should turn. He expressed astonishment that some painters still indulged in academic history painting rather than striving to capture the present on canvas. Manet was not alone in taking to heart the poet's injunction to paint Paris's "landscapes of stone" while strolling through the city—the French capital became one of the main subjects in Impressionist art (see ill. pp.83–7).

A NEW PARIS

Paris was transformed during the second half of the nineteenth century. Just a few days after his accession to the throne, Napoleon III initiated the first of the building works, on Boulevard de Strasbourg in the northeast part of the central district. And this was just the start of the *grands travaux*, a

comprehensive remodeling of the city under the supervision of Baron Haussmann, prefect of the Seine *département*. In his memoirs, Haussmann describes his task as follows: "A city, and even more so a capital, must befit its role within the country" (Muscheler).

Wide boulevards were driven through Paris's ancient and densely built-up central districts and lines of sight were opened up from north to south and east to west, punctuated by generously proportioned squares and public spaces (ill. pp.86–7). Under Napoleon and his energetic prefect, new districts were laid out around the edges of the city and the construction of administrative buildings and markets, a new opera house, and bridges across the Seine were ordered by the emperor. The city's famous parks, including the Bois de Boulogne in the west and the Bois de Vincennes in the east, also originated under this program of *grands travaux*.

Haussmann was also in charge of the modernization and expansion of the sewer system; indeed the results were so spectacular that tours of "underground Paris" were organized as part of the program of excursions offered during the second Paris Universal Exhibition of 1867.

The reasons for this comprehensive rebuilding of the city were on the one hand, the need for more living space (the number of inhabitants doubled to two million under the Second Empire), and on the other a desire to make the workers' districts in the center of Paris easier to control. Disturbances and rebellion had frequently originated in these districts, which had grown up haphazardly since the Middle Ages; the density with which the buildings were packed together made military intervention difficult. Haussmann wanted to put an end to uncontrolled growth. In keeping with his desire to make a name for himself in Paris, "controversial or otherwise," his renovation of the city failed to attract unmitigated enthusiasm.

▷ **Pierre-Auguste Renoir**, *Place Clichy*, ca. 1880.
Oil on canvas, 25½ x 21¼ in. (65 x 54 cm).
The Fitzwilliam Museum, Cambridge, England.

PAGES 80–81
Jean-François Raffaëlli, *Boulevard des Italiens* (detail), ca. 1900. Oil on canvas, 25 x 42¾ in. (63.5 x 108.5 cm). Galerie Daniel Malingue, Paris.

◁ **Claude Monet**, *Rue Saint-Denis during the Celebrations of 30 June 1878*, 1878. Oil on canvas, 30 x 20½ in. (76 x 52 cm). Musée des Beaux-Arts, Rouen, France.

Jean-François Raffaëlli, *Boulevard des Italiens*, ca. 1900. Oil on canvas, 25 x 42¾ in. (63.5 x 108.5 cm). Galerie Daniel Malingue, Paris.

Camille Pissarro, *Avenue de l'Opéra. Snow Effect. Morning*, 1898. Oil on canvas, 25½ x 32¼ in. (65 x 82 cm). Pushkin Museum, Moscow.

> *"For the out-and-out flâneur, for the passionate observer, it is an enormous pleasure to dwell among the masses, in the ebb and flow, in the movement, in the fleeting and infinite."*
> *Charles Baudelaire*

One particularly controversial aspect was the finances: the large-scale building works may have created jobs, but from 1860 forward they also landed Paris with debts as high as those of the entire French state. The work on the Île de la Cité, the medieval heart of Paris, also received criticism. Haussmann forced two-thirds of the inhabitants out and knocked down 20,000 buildings in the old city center.

In the stable economic climate of the nineteenth century, Paris became a city of pleasure—to be enjoyed not only by its inhabitants but also by tourists as the capital held no fewer than five world exhibitions between 1855 and 1900, luring crowds of visitors to the metropolis (see pp.56–7). After an aimless stroll, theater visit, or shopping trip in a sparkling new shrine to consumerism, there were plentiful cafés in which to relax.

Painters recorded aspects of the entire spectrum of life in the capital (ill. pp.88–9). Degas, Manet, and Renoir in particular were fond of depicting life on the boulevards, dance floors, concert platforms, and café terraces, capturing horse races, boating on the river, trips to the ballet, theater, and variety shows and recording the changing architectural face of the city (ill. pp.91–3).

One popular meeting place in which artists discussed Haussmann's plans and much else besides was Café Guerbois in Montmartre. Émile Zola and fellow writer Zacharie Astruc were regulars there, as were painters Antoine Guillemet, Félix Bracquemond, Constantin Guys, Henri Fantin-Latour, Manet, Degas, and Renoir. In the mid-1870s, the merry band was drawn to the Nouvelle Athènes on Place Pigalle, where Cézanne could also frequently be found, as the art dealer and writer Ambroise Vollard recalls, "Manet did not think particularly highly of the painter from Aix. The elegant, refined Parisian found that Cézanne the painter mirrored Cézanne the loose talker all too closely. And Cézanne would deliberately use vulgar expressions in order to offend the urbane Manet. On one occasion, Manet

Pierre-Auguste Renoir, *The Great Boulevards*, 1875.
Oil on canvas, 19¾ x 24 in. (50 x 61 cm). Private collection.

Berthe Morisot, *At the Ball*, 1875.
Oil on canvas, 24½ x 20½ in. (62 x 52 cm).
Musée Marmottan, Paris.

▷ Mary Cassatt, *Woman with a Pearl Necklace in a Loge*, 1879.
Oil on canvas, 32 x 23½ in. (81.3 x 59.7 cm). Philadelphia Museum of Art,
PA, U.S., Bequest of Charlotte Dorrance-Wright.

Edgar Degas, *Portrait of Edmond Duranty*, 1879.
Tempera, watercolor, and pastel on linen, 39¼ x 39¼ in. (100 x 100 cm).
The Burrell Collection, Glasgow, Scotland.

▷ Edgar Degas, *Miss La La at the Cirque Fernando*, 1879.
Oil on canvas, 46 x 30½ in. (116.8 x 77.5 cm).
The National Gallery, London.

enquired of Cézanne whether he was working on anything for the Salon exhibition and received the answer, 'Yes, a pot of sh**!'" (Vollard).

As well as indulging in friendly conversation, artists occasionally plied their trade in the Nouvelle Athènes, reflecting the seamier side of Parisian life. In 1876, Degas painted his friends the actress Ellen Andrée and the

artist Marcellin Desboutin drinking a glass of absinthe there (ill. p.92).

Another friend of Degas was the aristocrat Ludovic-Napoléon Lepic, who posed with his two daughters and their dog for *Place de la Concorde* (ill. pp.94–5). All three of them are cut off by the bottom edge of the picture. Lepic, cigar in mouth and umbrella clamped under his arm, has his face turned to

Édouard Manet, *Rue Mosnier with Pavers*, 1878.
Oil on canvas, 25¾ x 32 in. (65.5 x 81.5 cm). Private collection.

the right and his body bent forward in an apparent attempt to march out of the painting. His daughters, meanwhile, are facing the opposite direction. One is looking behind her father toward the left, while the other is staring at something outside the picture. At the left-hand edge a man in a top hat carrying a walking stick seems to be in the process of walking into the painting. The top half of the picture, where a wall marks the beginning of the Tuileries gardens, also has the appearance of having been cut off. The center of the picture, meanwhile,

Edgar Degas, *In a Café* or *Absinthe*, 1875.
Oil on canvas, 36¼ x 27 in. (92 x 68.5 cm). Musée d'Orsay, Paris.

This gloomy scene could have been taken from one of Émile Zola's novels: The outward appearance and facial expression of the two figures allows them to be interpreted as a metaphor for the darker side of modern life in the big city.

remains empty. As the art critic (and Nouvelle Athènes regular) Edmond Duranty (ill. p.90) observed, Degas succeeded with this picture in doing something photography could not yet do: taking a snapshot!

THE INFLUENCE OF PHOTOGRAPHY

From around the middle of the century, a new technology started to develop, photography, which came to exert a major influence on artistic creation and ways of seeing. Photographs had been shown at the Universal Exhibition of 1855 and were displayed at the Salon a few years later. The Parisian photographer Nadar became the talk of the town when he photographed the city from the air. The balloon he used, the largest of its day, was called *Le Géant* and was an attraction at the Universal Exhibition

93

◁ **Edgar Degas**, *The Orchestra at the Opera*, ca. 1870.
Oil on canvas, 22¼ x 18¼ in. (56.5 x 46.2 cm).
Musée d'Orsay, Paris.

Edgar Degas, *Jockeys in the Rain*, ca. 1886.
Pastel on paper, 18½ x 25 in. (47 x 63.5 cm).
The Burrell Collection, Glasgow, Scotland.

of 1867. It can be seen in the top right-hand corner of Manet's cityscape of the same year (ill. pp.56–7). Blurred figures and the cutting off of people and objects caught only partially by the camera lens started to become increasingly common in the work of painters as well.

Many artists, and the Impressionists in particular, used photographs as studies. Claude Monet, for example, used photographs as an alternative to preliminary sketches for his series of paintings of Rouen Cathedral.

Edgar Degas exhibited his photographic work at Nadar's studio on Boulevard des Capucines. In terms of faithful depiction of the subject, it was not long before photography was able to compete with painting. In the early stages, however, taking a photograph was barely less time-consuming than

PAGES 94–5
Edgar Degas, *Place de la Concorde*, 1875. Oil on canvas, 31 x 46½ in. (79 x 118 cm). Hermitage, St. Petersburg, Russia.

painting a picture. Only when exposure times became shorter could snapshot-like pictures of the kind that Degas had been creating on canvas since the 1870s be taken. However, Degas expressly distanced himself from any notion of spontaneity. "No art is less spontaneous than mine. What I do is the result of careful reflection and the study of old masters. Of inspiration, immediacy, and vitality I know nothing" (Blunden).

Degas did not have a lot of time for open-air painting as practiced and highly regarded by his colleagues. His horse racing and ballet scenes were painted in the studio. Only at the end of the 1870s, when his pictures of dancers had become popular collector's items, did he start setting up his easel at ballet rehearsals. As he confided to an acquaintance and passionate opera-goer, "I've painted so many of these dance rehearsals without ever having seen one that it makes me somewhat ashamed" (*Französische Meisterwerke*). The self-confessed studio painter seldom traveled to the location in question, even to perfect the depiction of movement, although he

97

would occasionally attend the races at Longchamp, the recently completed racetrack in the Bois de Boulogne (ill. p.97). This was a subject that also appealed to Nadar, who photographed the horses and jockeys in 1862.

"IT'S NOT JUST ABOUT PAINTING, YOU HAVE TO SELL TOO"

The rapid development—and recording by painters and photographers—of the modern metropolis was interrupted by the Franco-Prussian War of 1870–71. Napoleon III declared war on Prussia in July 1870 and by September the French army had surrendered. The German forces laid siege to Paris during the winter and the city eventually capitulated in January. Spring 1871 saw the rise of the Commune de Paris during which radical Socialists briefly gained control of the city. In the end an assault on the city was launched by French government troops and following what became known as the "Bloody Week," the Commune was defeated. A peace treaty was signed between France and the German Empire in May. Overshadowed by defeat in the war and the fighting in Paris, the Third Republic was born in a "mood of national remorse" (Droste-Hennings and Droste).

The painter Frédéric Bazille, an early supporter of Monet and other Impressionist painters, was killed in battle at Beaune-

la-Rolande in November 1870. Manet, Degas, and Morisot remained in Paris in spite of the war. Sisley and his future wife Marie also stayed behind at first—as a foreigner, Sisley had no fear of being called up to serve. Cézanne retreated south to L'Éstaque near Marseille when war broke out, while Monet and Pissarro escaped the draft by fleeing to London. Pissarro, already the father of three children, was hardly expecting his financial circumstances to improve as a result of the move, believing the prospects for Impressionist art in London to be even worse than in France. Monet's financial situation was also more than precarious. Since the birth of his son Jean in 1867, he had a family to feed. The repeated rejections by the Salon had not made it any easier for him to find buyers for his pictures. The landscape painter Daubigny repeatedly tried to help his fellow artists. As a member of the Salon jury he had spoken up for the entire group of Modernists until finally resigning from the 1870 Salon jury in protest against Monet's rejection.

In January 1871, Daubigny introduced Monet to the art dealer Paul Durand-Ruel, who had also fled to London and opened a gallery there. Durand-Ruel bought works by Monet and Pissarro—and at better prices than the painters were able to get in France—but was unable to sell them at his London exhibitions. Nevertheless, the artists placed hope in this sales channel and also introduced their colleagues Sisley and Degas to the dealer. Durand-Ruel bought several of their works. Perhaps with an eye on their hoped-for customers, Pissarro, Monet, and Sisley frequently opted for smaller formats (ill. pp.79, 98–101) during this time.

All three painters were interested in similar subjects during these years, the most common being riverscapes with brightly colored reflections. Their work of this period displays great similarities, including a sketch-like quality and a wide repertoire of brushstrokes, and in some cases it is difficult to identify the artist.

Were Paul Durand-Ruel's dealings the reason for a certain lack of interest in the 1872 Salon on the part of the Impressionists? Other than Manet, only Morisot and Renoir submitted works to the Salon jury—the latter without success. The activities of art dealers such as Durand-Ruel clearly represented competition for the Salon as a marketplace for art. Despite increasing liberalization from 1866 forward, the Salon had not been a particularly effective forum for the work of the Impressionist painters, even before the war. During the war and ensuing Commune the Salon system was suspended and had been reinstated without any major fundamental changes. On the contrary, the new superintendent of fine arts, Charles Blanc, had managed to give the forces of the establishment

even greater influence. As a result, the extremely rigorous jury of 1872 presided over the smallest Salon since the early days of the Second Empire. The most popular artist to be rejected was Courbet. Having been appointed president of the artists' commission during the Commune, he had been implicated in the scandal surrounding the destruction of that symbol of the Bonaparte dynasty—the column on Place Vendôme in Paris— and it has to be assumed that the jury's discussion of his work was influenced by this political context. Once again, numerous artists responded to the jury's harsh verdict with a petition. The request for another "Salon of the rejected," successful this time, was signed by over forty artists including Manet, Renoir, Pissarro, Cézanne, Jongkind, and Fantin-Latour. Overall, the situation in the years after France's lost war gave little cause for hope, and even the artists who were counting on Durand-Ruel rather than on the official channels were forced to realize that his affairs were going anything but well. Due to financial difficulties he eventually closed his London gallery in 1875.

Back in the 1860s the circle of artists who frequented Café Guerbois had already attempted to break free of the Salon system. In 1873, the critic Paul Alexis, himself a permanent fixture at Café Guerbois, wrote a number of articles in the

◁ **Alfred Sisley**, *The Seine at Bougival*, 1873.
Oil on canvas, 15 x 24½ in. (38 x 62 cm). Private collection.

Claude Monet, *Regatta at Argenteuil*, ca. 1872.
Oil on canvas, 19 x 29½ in. (48 x 75 cm). Musée d'Orsay, Paris.

journal *L'Avenir National* calling for the founding of an artists' cooperative. Organized along the lines of a trade union, it was intended that this group would be free of state patronage and would represent an alternative to the Salon.

Claude Monet was harboring similar plans: "What could we do? It's not just about painting, you have to sell, you have to live. The dealers didn't want us, yet we had to show our work. Where, though?" (*Impressionist Masterpieces*).

THE "SOCIÉTÉ ANONYME"

The quest for a suitable exhibition space was one thing, but the immediate task was to win over other artists. In 1873, Monet informed Pissarro of the difficulty he was having interesting other artists in his plan. Many regarded the idea of setting up an independent group with the aim of holding their own exhibitions as too risky. Degas also wrote to quite a number of artists and managed to convince several of them that the plan made sense. Finally, in December 1873, a group of thirty artists founded the "Société Anonyme des Artistes, Peintres, Sculpteurs, Graveurs, etc." Presenting themselves as a kind of limited liability corporation rather than a group of art lovers leaves no doubt as to the intention behind their association. The focus was on their economic interest: They had banded together in order to sell their work. This was reflected in their articles of incorporation, which were not a manifesto or statement of artistic intent but instead were based on the statutes of the Pontoise bakers' guild and regulated practical issues. Under these rules, each participant was required to pay into the kitty one-tenth of their sales proceeds plus an annual contribution of sixty francs.

In the end it was the photographer Nadar who came up with a suitable venue for the artists' exhibitions: his former studio on the bustling Boulevard des Capucines (ill. p.102). For their inaugural exhibition, over 150 pictures were hung in alphabetical order in this generous space. Unlike the Salon with its overflowing walls, the exhibitors were able to make do with two rows of paintings. The exhibition opened its doors sometime in advance of the Salon (so as not to be confused with the Salon des Refusés) on April 15, 1874. Over the next four weeks visitors were admitted between ten o'clock in the morning and six o'clock in the evening, while an additional evening session of eight until ten was designed to allow the working public to visit the show.

The thirty exhibitors were by no means all future Impressionists. Those whose work was displayed included

Alfred Sisley, *Regatta at Molesey*, 1874.
Oil on canvas, 26 x 36 in. (66 x 91.5 cm). Musée d'Orsay, Paris.

Nadar's studio at 35, Boulevard des Capucines, in a photograph dating from 1860. Bibliothèque Nationale, Paris.

Eugène Boudin, Félix Bracquemond, and Adolphe Félix Cals, all of whom exhibited regularly at the Salon. Others, such as Zacharie Astruc and Giuseppe de Nittis, were less well established. Fantin-Latour had decided not to participate. Cézanne showed *A Modern Olympia* (ill. pp.106–7), while Morisot presented *Mother and Sister Reading* (ill. p.77) and *The Cradle* (ill. p.103). Sisley, Monet, Renoir, and Pissarro all sold paintings at the exhibition, as did Degas, whom many critics praised for his excellent draftsmanship. Claude Monet showed twelve pieces including *Boulevard des Capucines* (ill. p.104), painted the previous year in the same studio in which it was now exhibited, and *Impression: Sunrise*, his now famous view of the port at Le Havre.

Numerous reviews were published of the first exhibition of the Société Anonyme thanks in part to the organizers' success in involving the press and keeping them informed of their plans. *Le Journal Amusant* and the satirical paper *Le Charivari* published negative reports on April 25. Probably the most quoted review is Louis Leroy's in *Le Charivari*, entitled "The Impressionists' Exhibition," which takes the form of a fictional conversation between two visitors, an academic painter and the critic himself. The critic repeatedly tries to convince the fictitious painter of the worth of the "impressions" on display—unsuccessfully,

it turns out, as the latter eventually succumbs to a kind of nervous breakdown. Leroy, in common with a number of other critics, found fault with the sketchy handling of works such as Pissarro's *Hoarfrost* (ill. p.105), Monet's *Boulevard des Capucines*, and above all, the same artist's *Impression: Sunrise*.

Leroy was not the only one to talk of "impressions"; the term was widely used at the time of the exhibition—by Monet too, of course, who later described how the name was chosen for his picture of the harbor sunrise: "I had submitted a picture painted from my window in Le Havre with the sun shining through the mist and a number of ship's masts rising up in the foreground…. I was asked its title for the catalog. As it couldn't very well be described as a view of Le Havre, I said, 'write *Impression*' " (*Impressionist Masterpieces*).

For a long time, the public image of the first Impressionist exhibition was shaped by Leroy's critique, as well as various other memorable negative verdicts (see ill. p.82). In fact, though, the tenor of opinion had changed. Leaving aside simple announcements of the exhibition, Belinda Thomson has counted forty-seven mentions in the press of the day—of those, twenty were positive, eighteen neutral, and just nine unambiguously negative.

Zola and Silvestre hailed the courage of the exhibitors, a number of critics praised the manageable size of the exhibition

> "She crushes petals on her palette and applies them to her canvas with delicate and dexterous strokes…. All of this harmonizes, coheres, and forms a whole, creating something living, exquisite, and enchanting that one intuitively perceives rather than sees."
>
> *Charles Ephrussi on Berthe Morisot*

and the way the works were hung, and many others spoke positively of the "impressions" on the walls of Nadar's studio. Both supporters and opponents of the exhibition tried to identify a leader of the group. Manet was frequently mentioned even though he had not even taken part.

With his figure paintings, Degas, who was of the same social class as Manet, was very different from the landscape-painting majority of exhibitors, and was, therefore, not particularly representative. In his 1878 study *Les Peintres Impressionistes*, Théodore Duret, a journalist, critic, essayist, and the first

Berthe Morisot, *The Cradle*, 1872.
Oil on canvas, 22 x 18 in. (56 x 46 cm).
Musée d'Orsay, Paris.

◁ **Claude Monet**, *Boulevard des Capucines*, 1873–74.
Oil on canvas, 31¼ x 23¼ in. (79.4 x 59 cm).
The Nelson-Atkins Museum of Art, Kansas City, MO, U.S.

Camille Pissarro, *Hoarfrost*, 1873.
Oil on canvas, 25½ x 36½ in. (65 x 93 cm).
Musée d'Orsay, Paris.

chronicler of the Impressionists, argued in favor of Monet: "If the word 'Impressionism' was found to be good and ultimately adopted as the name of a whole group of artists, then it was without doubt Claude Monet's painting that initially suggested it. Monet is the Impressionist par excellence" (*Impressionist Masterpieces*).

The Impressionists' daring exhibition was much discussed in the press—and the coverage was by no means exclusively negative. Neither were the visitors anywhere near as shocked as Leroy's alter ego. Just a few weeks after the exhibition, for example, the baritone Jean-Baptiste Faure (1830–1914) bought four works by Monet. In addition to Impressionist paintings he also collected the work of Corot, Delacroix, and Cézanne and had acquired Manet's *Spanish Singer* the previous year for 7,000 francs. Also, after this first exhibition Ernest Hoschedé (1837–91), the extremely wealthy heir to a textile factory and a regular purchaser of works by Monet, Pissarro, and Sisley, bought Monet's much-debated work *Impression: Sunrise* via Durand-Ruel.

Cézanne's nude *A Modern Olympia* (ill. pp.106–7) was one of the works that fared worst in the press. One critic even conjectured that the artist had painted it while suffering from delirium tremens. Of all the works on display, however, this one had to be loaned to the exhibition as it had already been acquired by Paul Gachet, a doctor and art collector from Auvers, just outside of Paris. As well as collectors of the first hour, around 3,500 members of the general public came to look around Nadar's studio. This is not to say the exhibition was a financial success. Costs had exceeded revenue and by the end of 1874 the Société Anonyme was finished.

FIRST DEFINITIONS

What made so many of the works exhibited in Nadar's studio "impressions" in the eyes of contemporaries (and indeed to the artists themselves)? In his review in the newspaper *Le Siècle* on April 29, 1874, Jules Castagnary explained why he

regarded Pissarro, Morisot, Monet, Sisley, Renoir, and Degas as "Impressionists": "They are Impressionists in the sense that they reproduce not the landscape but the sensory perceptions it evokes." And, after all, Monet's *Sunrise* was listed in the catalog as an "impression" rather than a "landscape." Why was the traditional terminology no longer adequate? Had paintings such as *Impression: Sunrise* ceased to be landscapes? What did the pictures that originated around the time of the first joint exhibition actually look like?

The hoarfrost in Pissarro's painting of the same name (ill. p.105) lies in dirty white patches on a landscape dominated by light ocher and green tones that is observed from a slightly elevated viewpoint. A number of trees project into the cloudy sky that occupies the top third of the picture. A countryman goes on his way carrying a bundle of twigs on his back. Pissarro composes the fields, trees, and solitary figure out of short side-by-side or overlapping brushstrokes, thereby remaining closely attached to the surface. This rapid, sketchy style was ideally suited to painting in the open air in constantly changing light conditions. The Impressionists did not paint exclusively outside, however, even if they were sometimes happy to let people think they did. Monet in particular was fond of declaring that he had no studio and always painted *en plein air* but in truth even he often started landscapes outdoors and later worked them up in the studio.

The critic Louis Leroy could not find a good word to say about Pissarro. When he shows his fictitious interlocutor the painter's *Hoarfrost* in his review of the first Impressionist exhibition, the academician initially removes his spectacles, convinced that dirty lenses were the reason the picture was making such a curious impression. The pictures Pissarro painted in the vicinity of Pontoise, a small town southwest of Paris in which he had settled in 1866, are very different from his early work (see, for example, ill. p.46). There are also clear differences between these later paintings and the kind of landscapes shown at the Salon, which were preferred not least by Leroy (ill. p.23). Pissarro increasingly abstained from creating a sense of depth in his pictures. Horizontal and vertical lines continued to cut through his landscapes but the dramatic chiaroscuro disappeared. Varied brushstrokes applied freely side by side in clear, light shades allow simple shapes to emerge, whether a bundle of twigs, a horse-drawn cart, or a farmer's wife (ill. pp.108–9).

In Monet's *Boulevard des Capucines* (ill. p.104), two gentlemen wearing top hats look down onto the street from a balcony, although they are largely cut off by the right-hand edge of the picture. The passersby on the lively boulevard and the houses and trees that line it are conveyed with rapid brushstrokes. The

Paul Cézanne, *A Modern Olympia*, 1873–74.
Oil on canvas, 18 x 22 in. (46 x 56 cm). Musée d'Orsay, Paris.

Camille Pissarro, *Kitchen Gardens at L'Hermitage, Pontoise,* 1874.
Oil on canvas, 21¼ x 25½ in. (54 x 65.1 cm).
National Gallery of Scotland, Edinburgh.

▷ **Camille Pissarro,** *Ploughed Earth,* 1874.
Oil on canvas, 19¼ x 25¼ in. (49 x 64 cm).
Pushkin Museum, Moscow.

viewer observes the scene from more or less the height of the balcony but no clear perspective is discernible. Forms and the picture space emerge from the surface through color contrasts but they are not delimited by outlines. Graphic elements play only a subsidiary role, while unmixed colors applied in short brushstrokes comprise the main means of pictorial organization. Only when viewing the picture from a distance do the lines and dots merge into one another, allowing the eye to make out the street, houses, and figures.

In Berthe Morisot's view of Paris painted from the Trocadéro, a semicircular patch of grass separates the foreground from the cityscape in the upper half of the picture (ill. pp.110–11). Compared with Manet's view painted from the same spot (ill. pp.56–7), Morisot's takes a broader sweep and seems less compressed. A few individual figures and details stand out against the patches of color representing lawns and rows of trees that show the influence of Morisot's teacher Corot. The figures and coaches in the middle ground of the picture are merely suggested with a few rapid strokes.

Not only did Morisot change her style of painting at the beginning of the 1870s, she also started to take a new direction in terms of composition and palette. Her Isle of Wight harbor scene of 1875 (ill. p.112) has a two-dimensional character, with brushstrokes that are even freer than those in her Paris view. In a later work probably shown at the Impressionists' fifth group exhibition in 1880, this two-dimensional and sketch-like quality is taken even further: two elegantly dressed women are enjoying a boat trip on the lake in the Bois de Boulogne in Paris

on a summer's day (ill. p.113). Their boat forms a diagonal across the picture and their bodies are cut off by the bottom and left edges of the painting. The faces and clothing of the two women, the surface of the water, and the narrow strip of shoreline along which a horse-drawn coach is traveling are rendered with dense strokes and dabs of the brush. Morisot refrains from giving any of the figures of objects in the painting a clear outline or reproducing their true colors. While Morisot captures the mood of a sunny day through her sketchy handling of the subject, Monet conveys the hustle and bustle of a city street on an overcast day and Pissarro conveys the stillness and chill of the fields. They all attach more importance to the overall effect and specific atmosphere of a brief moment with its particular light and play of colors than to the detail. In keeping with this focus on mood, the titles of the Impressionists' pictures reveal relatively little about their actual subjects—*Little Girl in a Blue Armchair* (Cassatt), *Summer's Day*, or *Sunrise*. To return to what Monet said about *Impression: Sunrise*, "It couldn't very well be

described as a view of Le Havre." The precise subject matter was secondary to the impression experienced by the artist and artistic traditions retreated into the background in favor of what was actually seen.

ARGENTEUIL

Nearly all the Impressionist painters worked for a shorter or longer period of time at Argenteuil, which consequently features in numerous pictures of the 1870s—such as Monet's famous *Poppy Field at Argenteuil* (ill. pp.114–15). Situated just a few miles south of Paris and reachable by railroad or river, this

PAGES 110–11
Berthe Morisot, *View of Paris from the Trocadéro*, 1872.
Oil on canvas, 18 x 32 in. (45.9 x 81.4 cm).
Museum of Art, Santa Barbara, CA, U.S., Gift of Mrs. Hugh N. Kirkland.

Berthe Morisot, *The Isle of Wight*, 1875.
Oil on canvas, 14¼ x 19 in. (36 x 48 cm). Private collection.

village on the right bank of the Seine was a popular destination for excursions. Monet moved there in 1873 and a number of other artists followed suit including Sisley and Renoir. Monet painted a number of pictures of the bridge over which the railroad line to Argenteuil passed. In the version of this subject that now hangs in the Musée d'Orsay in Paris (ill. p.116), the bridge cuts diagonally through the picture and the gray smoke from the train rises into the cloudy sky. In other versions of the same subject, Monet left out the vegetation along the bank of the river in the foreground and paid particular attention to the variable light conditions.

Numerous series of pictures emerged over the next few years as a result of Monet's interest in capturing the same motif in changing atmospheric conditions and at different times of the day and year. In 1873, Pierre-Auguste Renoir painted a picture

of his fellow painter at work in Argenteuil (see ill. p.117), where they often painted together as before in Bougival. In summer 1874, they were joined by Édouard Manet, who, Monet reports, conspiratorially passed on what he thought was a piece of good advice. As Manet was painting a portrait of the Monet family one day, Renoir joined them, took up a canvas and started painting the same subject. After seeing the results, Manet took Monet aside and said to him, "Monet, you're a friend of Renoir's, why don't you advise him to take up a different career? You can see for yourself that he's not cut out for painting" (Krems).

Manet also painted his friend Monet at work. The latter often painted riverscapes from his boat, an idea he probably borrowed from Daubigny of the Barbizon circle, who as early as the 1850s had painted landscapes along the shores of the

Oise and Seine rivers from his houseboat. As his picture *Monet Painting in his Studio Boat* (ill. p.118), which hangs today in the Neue Pinakothek in Munich, testifies, Manet continued his experiments with an Impressionist style of painting under the influence of Monet, his junior by several years. Manet's portrait of a couple sitting on a landing stage (see ill. p.119) also displays freer brushwork, particularly in the rendering of

In the year of the first Impressionist exhibition, Manet submitted four works to the Salon, only two of which met with the favor of the jury: a watercolor and an oil painting entitled *The Railway* (ill. p.120), which now hangs in the National Gallery of Art in Washington, DC. *The Railway* was painted in Manet's new studio on Rue Saint-Pétersbourg, just a stone's throw from the Pont de l'Europe and Gare Saint-Lazare (see ill. p.122), the

Berthe Morisot, *Summer's Day*, 1879.
Oil on canvas, 18 x 29½ in. (45.7 x 75.2 cm). The National Gallery, London.

the landscape in the top half of the picture. Whereas he had previously worked with strong contrasts of light and shade, he now made greater use of color as a way of modeling his figures. The figure of Monet at work in his boat, for example, only stands out from his surroundings due to the brightness of his clothing and Camille's face and attire are merely suggested. The water of the Seine is rendered with blue, white, and grayish horizontal brushstrokes. "One doesn't paint a landscape, the sea, or a figure," stressed Manet on more than one occasion, "one paints the impression of a particular time of day." Despite uttering comments of this kind and despite his excursions to Argenteuil and experimentation with an Impressionist style of painting, Manet never participated in the exhibitions organized by Monet and his circle. On the contrary, despite mixed success, he continued to submit pictures to the Salon each year.

city's largest train station. Unsurprisingly for Manet, who was used to negative comments, the critics did not hold back. One of their main objections concerned the title. The picture shows neither railroad nor station (although the steam in the background at least hints at a locomotive). A comparison with Monet's handling of the subject emphasizes the difference in focus of the two works. In Monet's painting the steaming locomotive, the very embodiment of technology and progress, is the protagonist whereas the human beings in the station remain sketchy (see ill. p.122).

Manet, on the other hand, concentrates on the portrayal of two figures. A woman in a blue dress sits in front of a metal fence with a book on her knee and returns the gaze of the viewer, who by now is most probably familiar with her face as it is once again that of Victorine Meurent. Next to her stands a

Claude Monet, *Poppy Field at Argenteuil*, 1873.
Oil on canvas, 19¾ x 25½ in. (50 x 65 cm).
Musée d'Orsay, Paris.

In this famous painting, Monet dispenses almost
completely with outlines—see, for example, the two
figures in the middle ground on the left. That he was
concerned primarily with conveying a visual impression
is evident not least in the way he handles the poppies. An
impeccably balanced color scheme is developed from the
disproportionately large spots of color in the foreground.
Visible in the background is Monet's house near Argenteuil
on the Seine. The figures in the foreground are his wife,
Camille, and six-year-old son, Jean.

Claude Monet, *The Railway Bridge at Argenteuil*, ca. 1873–74.
Oil on canvas, 21¾ x 28¼ in. (55 x 72 cm).
Musée d'Orsay, Paris.

▷ **Pierre-Auguste Renoir**, *Monet Painting in his Garden in Argenteuil*, 1873.
Oil on canvas, 18 x 23½ in. (46 x 60 cm).
Wadsworth Atheneum Museum of Art, Hartford, CT, U.S.

small child in a white dress who looks through the metal bars toward the railroad track. In addition to the title, viewers were also disturbed by the handling. The brushwork is clearly visible, and explains why many critics associated Manet with the Impressionists. Even during the first Impressionist exhibition his name had continually been mentioned, despite his lack of involvement. The fact that two of his pictures had been rejected by the 1874 Salon jury may also have encouraged the perception of him as leader of the Impressionists. Furthermore, the marriage of his friend Berthe Morisot to his brother Eugène in December 1874 would have done nothing to distance him from the Impressionists in the eyes of the general public.

Manet's Salon successes, however, remained few. In 1875, he cautiously submitted just one work, which was accepted but heavily criticized. The following year the jury yet again did not see fit to show anything by him, whereupon he decided to open his studio to the public. According to Zola,

more than 10,000 visitors passed through its doors in two weeks. While his *Olympia* had been the art scandal of the 1865 season, twelve years later it was another work of Manet's that threw the Parisian art world into a frenzy: *Nana* (ill. p.121), with its provocative history-painting dimensions. Standing prominently in the center of the picture, in her petticoat, is a prostitute who powders her nose and stares self-assuredly at the viewer. Seated behind her on the right, cut off by the edge of the picture, is a gentleman in top hat and tails, a figure Manet may have added to the picture after reading Zola's 1877 novel *L'Assommoir*. In Zola's work Nana is the neglected daughter of a laundress who turns to prostitution. This time it was not only the subject of the picture (whose palette is reminiscent of Rococo art) and the free handling, but also the choice of model that was the undoing of this painter who was ever willing to subvert tradition. The model was "the well-known mistress of a foreign prince" (Rewald), namely Henriette Hauser, an operetta star of dubious repute who had taken up with the Prince of Orange. Manet reacted to his rejection from the Salon by displaying the picture in the window of a junk shop on the Boulevard des Capucines. The remark, "I paint what I see, not what others like to see" has been attributed to him perhaps unreliably, but it is no less true that Manet continued to provoke from both inside and outside the Salon and was undaunted by any criticism.

"IMPRESSIONISTS" OR "INDEPENDENT ARTISTS"?

At the same time that Manet was holding his studio exhibition in April 1876, nineteen artists were displaying a total of 252 oil paintings, pastels, watercolors, drawings, and etchings under the simple title "2ième Exposition de Peinture." They had hired Paul Durand-Ruel's gallery on Rue Le Pelletier for the occasion. The Impressionist core of the group provided around one hundred of the pieces. Degas showed twenty-four works,

Morisot seventeen, and Sisley eight landscapes. Of the twelve works presented by Pissarro, two were already owned by Durand-Ruel at the time of the exhibition, Monet had borrowed back a number of his eighteen pictures from Jean-Baptiste Faure, and six of Renoir's fifteen works were already in the possession of Victor Choquet, who was a very regular collector, albeit with a smaller budget.

Despite these sales to collectors and dealers and a few successes at the exhibition—Monet's portrait of his wife *La Japonaise (Camille Monet in Japanese Costume)* (ill. p.69) caused a stir and found a buyer prepared to part with 2,000 francs for it—the Impressionists' financial situation remained precarious. Neither was Manet's solo show particularly successful from a sales point of view. A few months after the second exhibition, Eugène Manet wrote to his wife Berthe Morisot, "The entire painting community is in difficulty. The dealers are overloaded. Édouard [Manet] is talking of cutting down and giving up his studio. Let's hope buyers show up

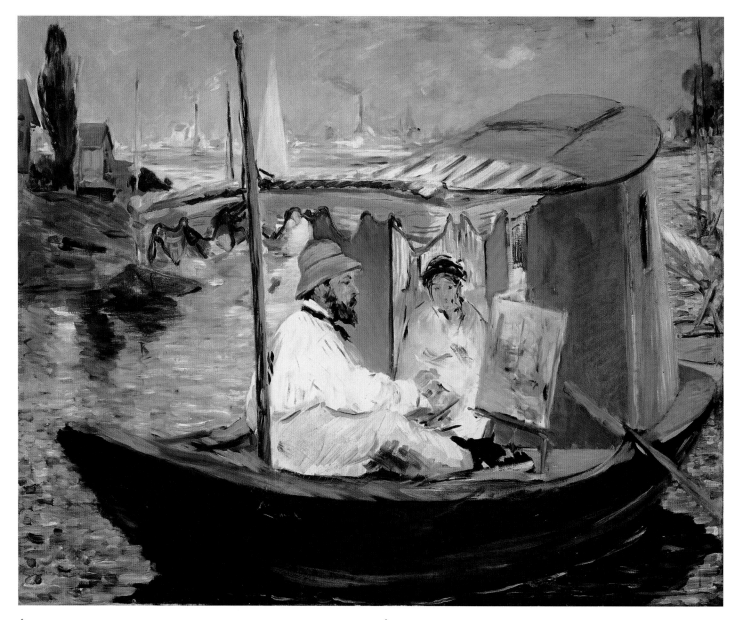

Édouard Manet, *Monet Painting in his Studio Boat*, 1874.
Oil on canvas, 32½ x 41 in. (82.7 x 105 cm). Bayerische
Staatsgemäldesammlungen, Neue Pinakothek, Munich, Germany.

▷ **Édouard Manet**, *Argenteuil*, 1874.
Oil on canvas, 58¾ x 45¼ in. (149 x 115 cm).
Musée des Beaux-Arts, Tournai, Belgium.

again soon. For the time being, though, things are not looking good" (Rewald).

Running through the reviews of the second Impressionist exhibition was again a common theme. One of the most negative critiques was penned by Albert Wolf for the *Figaro*, "After the opera house fire another disaster has befallen Rue Le Pelletier. An exhibition of so-called painting has opened at Durand-Ruel. Unsuspecting passersby, drawn by the beflagged façade, enter the premises and meet with a fearsome spectacle: five or six lunatics blinded by ambition, including one woman, have put their work on display here. Many visitors are seized by fits of laughter at the sight of their sorry efforts and for my part I experienced a convulsion of the heart. These self-appointed artists call themselves subversives, Impressionists. They take up canvas, paint, and brush, apply a few colors at random next

to one another and then sign the thing.... Pissarro must be made to understand that trees are not violet, the sky is not the color of fresh butter, and in no country on Earth are the things he paints to be seen" (Rewald).

As well as writing a review of that year's official Salon, in which he criticized the rejection of Manet, Émile Zola also covered the Impressionists' 1876 exhibition. Whereas he expressed approval of the work of Morisot, Pissarro, Renoir, and Sisley, he found that Degas spoiled most of his paintings in the finishing. Zola saw Monet as the "undisputed leader of the group." He was not, however, able to summon up any enthusiasm for the work of Gustave Caillebotte, who exhibited with the Impressionists for the first time in 1876. Its trueness to life struck him as bearing too great a resemblance to photography and thus as "anti-artistic." The critic Edmond

Édouard Manet, *The Railway*, 1873.
Oil on canvas, 36¾ x 44 in. (93.3 x 111.5 cm).
National Gallery of Art, Washington, DC.

▷ Édouard Manet, *Nana*, 1877.
Oil on canvas, 60½ x 45¼ in. (154 x 115 cm).
Hamburger Kunsthalle, Hamburg, Germany.

Duranty had more time for Degas and Caillebotte (and Manet too) and compared their work to looking through a window, "Depending on whether we are close to the window or further away from it, and depending on whether we are sitting or standing, the frame cuts up the scene in the most unexpected, ever-changing way, creating continual diversion as well as something unhoped for—the enormous charm of reality" (*Impressionist Masterpieces*).

Gustave Caillebotte, who was from a well-to-do family, was largely responsible for guaranteeing that the third Impressionist exhibition was able to go ahead. In 1876, he had stipulated in his will that in the event of his death a sufficient sum should be made available to the Impressionist painters to finance their next exhibition. As it turned out, Caillebotte, who was only twenty-eight, did not die and was able to support

the project personally by paying the rent for the exhibition space. The exhibition was held in an empty apartment not far from Paul Durand-Ruel's gallery. Prior to the exhibition, explicitly announced this time as the Impressionist Exhibition, a number of artists, prominent among whom was Degas, fought to exclude those artists who also exhibited at the Salon. In the end, works by eighteen artists, including Boudin, de Nittis, Astruc, Bracquemond, and Guillaumin, were shown. Berthe Morisot took part, Monet presented thirty-five works, Renoir thirty-one, Sisley twenty-seven, Degas twenty-five, and Pissarro twenty-two.

As in the previous year's exhibition, the 230 pictures on display included quite a few loans from collectors and gallerists. The most important lender was Ernest Hoschedé, who was nevertheless facing bankruptcy. The Impressionists' public

Claude Monet, *La Gare Saint-Lazare*, 1877.
Oil on canvas, 29¾ x 41 in. (75.5 x 104 cm).
Musée d'Orsay, Paris.

▷ Gustave Caillebotte, *Le Pont de L'Europe*, 1876.
Oil on canvas, 49¼ x 70¾ in. (125 x 180 cm).
Musée du Petit Palais, Geneva, Switzerland.

relations' work proved more successful than before. Eight thousand people visited the exhibition in Rue Le Pelletier and some fifty reviews appeared in the press.

Cézanne, whom Caillebotte had managed to persuade to participate this year, again came in for heavy criticism. As in his response to the first Impressionist exhibition, the critic Louis Leroy vented his feelings in the newspaper *Le Charivari*, this time singling out Cézanne's portrait of the proud collector of fifty of the artist's works, Victor Choquet (ill. p.125). Caillebotte's six pictures, including an interior showing floor planers at work (which was rejected by the Salon), and *Le Pont de L'Europe* (ill. p.123), attracted a lot of attention but irritated critics with their "flat" handling and emphatically perspective-based construction. In *Le Pont de L'Europe* a strolling man, who is apparently turning to talk to a lady with a parasol, and a worker leaning against the railings on the right-hand side are the two main figures and initially draw the viewer's gaze.

The iron bridge had spanned the Gare Saint-Lazare railroad line since 1868. It fascinated not only Caillebotte, whose studio and apartment were close by, but also de Nittis and Monet. Monet also showed his versions of it at the third Impressionist exhibition and three of his works using the train station as their subject were already part of Caillebotte's rapidly growing collection (see ill. p.122).

Caillebotte bought Renoir's large-format canvas *Dance at the Moulin de la Galette* (ill. pp.126–7) in 1879 and even incorporated it into his self-portrait painted two years later (ill. pp.124–5). Modern in subject matter, innovative in terms of handling, and at 51½ x 69 in. (131 x 175 cm), ambitious in size, Renoir presents a portrait of the youth of Montmartre. Captured with vivacious brushstrokes and dappled with light that shines through the leaves of the garden's trees, an animated crowd of young people are drinking, flirting, and amusing themselves on the dance floor. While half of Paris seems to have gathered in this popular

café on Montmartre, in reality, friends of the artist posed for many of the figures.

Not only did 1879 bring Renoir a pleasing volume of sales, the group exhibition (held on Avenue de l'Opéra) also made a profit for the first time. The American painter Mary Cassatt, who had joined the "independent artists" (as they began to call themselves in 1879) after their third exhibition, invested in two of her colleagues' pictures: one by Monet and one by Degas, the latter having invited the young painter to join them after she had been turned down for the Salon. After previously ejecting those artists who also exhibited at the Salon, Degas had gotten his way again by persuading the group to give up the label "Impressionists" and refer to themselves instead as a "group of independent artists." He for one by no means regarded himself as an Impressionist and had already made clear to his friend the painter James Tissot at the time of the first exhibition in 1874 that he felt stronger ties with Realism: "I'm quite excited. I'm working away seriously and, I believe, highly successfully…. The Realist movement no longer needs to do battle with others. It is, it exists, and it must show separately. There should be a Salon of the Realists" (*Impressionist Masterpieces*).

This had still not happened by 1879, although in addition to Degas and Cassatt, the "independent artists" were able to count Caillebotte, Monet, Pissarro, and Marie and Félix Bracquemond among their number. Monet and Pissarro (who enjoyed some success with a series of painted fans) made the biggest contributions to the exhibition. Monet exhibited (or more accurately arranged to be exhibited) a whole series of older paintings that Caillebotte requested on loan from various collectors. He himself had withdrawn from public life following the death of his wife at the beginning of the year and did not attend the exhibition. Morisot was expecting a baby and did not participate and Degas presented just eight pictures rather than the twenty-five he had announced in the catalog. Cézanne, Renoir, and Sisley tried their luck with the Salon, of which they had high hopes following the repeated election successes of the Republicans. The rules had changed very little, however, and consequently only Renoir's works cleared the jury hurdle.

Paul Cézanne, *Portrait of Victor Choquet*, 1876–77.
Oil on canvas, 18 x 14½ in. (45.7 x 36.8 cm). Private collection.

◁ **Gustave Caillebotte**, *Self-Portrait in Front of "Dance at the Moulin de la Galette,"* ca. 1879. Oil on canvas, 35½ x 45¼ in. (90 x 115 cm). Private collection.

"I wish the necessary sum to be taken out of my estate and used to organize an exhibition of the so-called Impressionists in 1878 under the best possible conditions. I am unable to provide a precise estimate of the sum at present, but it is likely to be in the region of 30,000 to 40,000 francs. The painters who are to participate in this exhibition are: Degas, Monet, Renoir, Cézanne, Sisley, and Berthe Morisot."

Gustave Caillebotte, from the beginning of his will of November 1876

> "As he has no memory of the pressures artists all too often put themselves under, he allows himself to be carried away by his subject and above all by the surroundings in which he finds himself.... 'He paints the Moulin de la Galette'? For a period of six months he takes up residence there, makes contact with members of this little world with a life all of its own..., and in the midst of the commotion reproduces the wild movements of this popular dance café with dizzying élan."

Edmond Renoir on his brother Pierre-Auguste

Pierre-Auguste Renoir, *Dance at the Moulin de la Galette*, 1876.
Oil on canvas, 51½ x 69 in. (131 x 175 cm).
Musée d'Orsay, Paris.

Renoir loved the cheerful, easygoing atmosphere at this popular café where the youth of Montmartre gathered to dance on Sunday evenings. Despite its large dimensions, this homage to beauty and light was no studio picture but was painted on location. The models were from the artist's circle of friends and acquaintances.

THE COLOR OF SOUND—IMPRESSIONIST MUSIC

Parallel to the developments occurring in the visual arts, the term "Impressionism" was also used in reference to the compositional innovations that dominated French music, in particular, during the decades immediately before and after the turn of the century. Composers, like painters, were concerned with capturing or creating the sensory perceptions emanating from a subject, usually a picture of nature—this time by musical means.

Claude Debussy with bass clarinet, photographed by Pierre Louÿs in the latter's apartment in 1894.

In 1884, a new forum for art held its inaugural exhibition. Artists of every imaginable persuasion took part in the enormous Salon des Indépéndants. The organizers dispensed with a jury, an integral part of the official Salon, and left the task of judging the works to the public. Academy, jury, the awarding of prizes—many painters and sculptors (and by no means only Impressionists) had turned their backs on these aspects of the official art world by the late nineteenth century. However, artists continued to compete for the Prix de Rome, which had been created in the 17th century and was conferred by the royal academies of the various arts.

The competition was also open to musicians and was won in 1884 by Claude Debussy (1862–1918). The winner was entitled to stay at the Académie de France in Rome, with expenses paid. The young composer traveled to Rome and, as scholarship holders were required to do, sent home the works he wrote there. One such delivery, designed to provide evidence of his progress to date, was made in 1887. Those at the Academy were anything but taken with his orchestral piece *Printemps*, however: "Not only does M. Debussy commit the error of wandering off into the superficial or banal," felt the learned critics, "but he also displays an excessive propensity towards the exotic. It is not difficult to detect his predilection for tonal color but its excessive use often causes him to forget the importance of clear forms and sharpness of contour. We fervently hope that he will be on his guard and will not allow himself to be carried away by the vagaries of Impressionism, which represents the most dangerous enemy of truth in art" (Nichols). Within the context of Impressionist painting there was nothing new about an artist being accused of emphasizing tonal color at the expense of form. Within a musical context, however, there was, and by the turn of the century the term "Impressionism" no longer simply denoted a specific group of painters; it also pertained to wider areas of culture.

In *Printemps*, Debussy developed his own style of composition and instrumentation that departed from the traditional principles and practices of European music. His melodic figures do not develop. Instead, concurrent themes intertwine, motifs appear out of nowhere and are then superseded just as quickly, and rhythmic stresses are masked. Formlessness was a criticism that plagued Debussy for much of his creative life. Two works that were especially closely associated by music critics of the day with the term "Impressionism" were his instrumental work *Prélude à l'après-midi d'un faune*, inspired by a poem by Stéphane Mallarmé, and his set of "symphonic sketches," *La mer*, that premiered in 1894 and 1905, respectively. A comparison between music and painting was encouraged by a shared scientific basis adopted by composers and painters alike. Many Impressionist painters discussed theories from the field of optics and reacted to its new discoveries in their work.

Other scientific discoveries had a major impact on music theory. The German physicist Hermann Helmholtz (1821–94), for instance, conducted research not only into color contrasts but also into the properties of musical notes, more specifically tone color, whose characteristics he tried to explain by the number, nature, and intensity of their overtones. The cover of the score of *La mer* also hints at another source of inspiration for Debussy. The first edition bore an image from one of the best known works of Asian art at that time: Katsushika Hokusai's color woodblock print *The Great Wave of Kanagawa* (ill. p.68). Clearly the art of the Far East filled not only Monet, Renoir, and Degas with enthusiasm but some of their contemporaries in the musical world as well.

Unlike Debussy, Maurice Ravel (1875–1937), his junior by thirteen years, started his career anything other than brilliantly. He tried for the Prix de Rome five times without success. Public, if not academic, success came when he was in his mid-twenties. With works such as *Jeux d'eau* (premiered 1902), Ravel emphasized his talent for compositional innovation. His study in instrumentation, entitled *Boléro*, written in three-quarter time, which received its first concert performance in 1930, would later become one of the most frequently performed works in the orchestral repertoire.

Cover of the first edition of the score of Debussy's *La mer*, Paris, 1905. Color print based on the woodblock *The Great Wave of Kanagawa* by Katsushika Hokusai, ca. 1830. Bibliothèque Nationale, Paris.

Luc Albert Moreau, *Ravel Conducting "Boléro,"* 1928. Drawing.

And just as it had been by the Impressionist paintings, public opinion was now divided by Debussy's compositions, particularly his one and only opera. *Pelléas et Mélisande*, an opera in five acts that premiered in 1902, is based on a play by the Symbolist writer Maurice Maeterlinck (1862–1949), and deals with the doomed, forbidden love of two half-brothers for a mysterious woman. Not only was the material modern— Debussy flouted convention by placing an emphasis on a formally freer version of *Sprechstimme* (a form of voice delivery midway between speech and song) rather than prominent arias and choruses.

Ravel and Debussy are considered the main exponents of Impressionist music due to stylistic innovations such as an emphasis on tonal color, flowing, wave-like melodies, and generally free harmonies. Debussy, however, considered the label to be completely inappropriate. This disjunction between the way artists see themselves and the way they are seen by others with regard to labels of this kind is something Debussy had in common with a number of the "Impressionist" painters. For his part, Ravel could not understand why his *Boléro* was so popular, "My masterpiece? *Boléro* of course. It's just a pity it contains no music."

IV. HETEROGENEITY BECOMES ESTABLISHED

HETEROGENEITY BECOMES ESTABLISHED

By 1886 the "Independent" or "Impressionist" artists had planned and held four additional exhibitions, yet during the 1880s as a whole they became less and less what one could call an established group, let alone a unified one. The individuals making up those "Independent Artists," who announced the fifth exhibition in 1880, were again different from those of the year before. Like Renoir and Sisley, Monet too made no contribution this time, instead submitting works to the official Salon, a step to which Degas in particular took exception. Cézanne, harshly reviewed in 1877, no longer had the heart to exhibit. But Pissarro and Gauguin—who was invited by Pissarro—were represented, and Cassatt, Morisot, Degas, Caillebotte, Guillaumin, Raffaëlli, and the Bracquemonds were also among the eighteen painters who exhibited in April at the Rue des Pyramides rooms (ill. pp.136–7). Of the thirteen works by Paul Gauguin, it was *Study of a Nude. Suzanne Sewing* (ill. p.133) that won the particular admiration of the critic Joris-Karl Huysmans, a close friend of Zola: "Here is a girl of our own day, not posing for an audience, not sensual, not in a state of strong emotion, quite simply concentrating on mending her clothes" (Dippel). Zola himself had forsaken art criticism to concentrate on his novels. The defender of Impressionism had lost interest in the cause, but he did ensure that Huysmans took on the task of reporting on the Salon for the daily *Le Voltaire* and thus followed in Zola's own footsteps, even in terms of what he said.

The year 1881 saw considerable tension generated by the preparations for the upcoming Impressionist exhibition, of which Pissarro and Caillebotte, as before, were the most forceful advocates. Degas had done all in his power to persuade his disciples to take part. Figure painters, such as Jean-Louis Forain and Jean-François Raffaëlli, Eugène Vidal, and Federico Zandomeneghi, were all invited by Degas and all accepted gratefully. This did not please everyone, however. Caillebotte regarded Degas and his circle of friends as troublemakers and felt they should be excluded; but to this Pissarro objected. The discord did not prevent the opening, in April 1881, of the sixth exhibition of independent artists—held, like the 1874 exhibition, at 35, Boulevard des Capucines, but in a smaller suite of rooms. Critics were disturbed by the show's notable lack of balance; the greatest number of paintings had been contributed by Raffaëlli

(1850–1924, ill. p.85), who was one of a total of eight from the Degas circle among the thirteen exhibitors. Degas himself sent only six pictures, but attracted considerable attention with his wax statue of a female dancer—the first (and only) sculpture of his ever to be exhibited in public. Morisot and Cassatt participated; Gauguin showed eight pictures, some of them loaned for the purpose by his first collectors, Degas and de Bellio. In spite of the differences of opinion, Pissarro too took part. Monet, Renoir, and Sisley, however, sent work to the Salon this year again, and did not contribute to the exhibition.

Ever since the second exhibition, the critics' interest had been engaged by the rift between the "Colorists" and the "Realists," and now they were already predicting the end for the Impressionists—even though, in the wake of the sixth exhibition, the actual concept of Impressionism seemed less clear to them than ever. In oversimplified terms, the time was approaching when a choice would have to be made: between landscape painting and color, as represented by Monet and Renoir on the one hand, and the figure and academic drawing à la Degas on the other. In their endeavor to ensure a distinctive profile for their group exhibitions, the Impressionist painters ended up behaving no less exclusively than had the Salon: It was announced that at the next exhibition, in 1882, only nine artists would be represented. Raffaëlli was excluded, this at the urging of Gauguin and Caillebotte in particular. Degas refused to be involved if Raffaëlli was not going to be there, Gauguin dropped out, and Renoir withdrew because of illness. Morisot, her husband, Eugène Manet, and Pissarro tried to pour oil on the troubled waters. In the end Durand-Ruel took charge of the register, and after weeks of correspondence—Monet made his participation conditional on Renoir's, Cézanne wrote to Pissarro saying he had nothing to send, and so on—he succeeded in setting up another exhibition. Most of the works shown came

▷ **Paul Gauguin**, *Study of a Nude. Suzanne Sewing*, 1880.
Oil on canvas, 45¼ x 31½ in. (115 x 80 cm).
Ny Carlsberg Glyptotek, Copenhagen.

PAGES 130–31
Pierre-Auguste Renoir, *Luncheon of the Boating Party* (detail), 1880–81.
Oil on canvas, 51 x 68 in. (129.5 x 172.7 cm).
The Phillips Collection, Washington, DC.

Armand Guillaumin, *Landscape in the Île-de-France*, ca. 1878.
Oil on canvas, 19¾ x 23½ in. (50 x 60 cm). Galerie Daniel Malingue, Paris.

from the dealer's stock. Thanks to thirty Monets, twenty-seven Sisleys, and twenty-five paintings and gouaches by Pissarro, landscapes dominated the 1882 show—and once again the critics were perplexed. Renoir exhibited twenty-five pictures, Morisot nine. Caillebotte had put in seventeen works, including *Boulevard from above* (ill. p.134) and *Top-Hatted Gentleman on a Balcony above the Boulevard Haussmann* (ill. p.135), paintings in

PAGE 134
Gustave Caillebotte, *Boulevard from above*, 1880.
Oil on canvas, 25½ x 21¼ in. (65 x 54 cm). Private collection.

PAGE 135
Gustave Caillebotte, *Top-Hatted Gentleman on a Balcony above the Boulevard Haussmann*, 1880.
Oil on canvas, 45¾ x 35 in. (116.5 x 89 cm). Christie's, London.

which he indulged his taste for spectacular foreshortenings; Ernest Chesneau called him a "lover of strange perspectives" (Caillebotte). The choices made for the exhibition that opened in the Rue Saint-Honoré on March 1, 1882 reminded observers of the 1874 exhibition, thus earning reviews that were not all favorable. In the *Paris* journal, Jacques de Biez criticized the Impressionists, who in his view had failed to progress: "Impressionists they wanted to be, and Impressionists they have remained. But then of course in the broader sense of the term we are all Impressionists. In every art, the 'impression' has a role to play, because it gives the initial stimulus.... One is no artist, however, if one fails to transcend this initial 'impression' made on the senses and goes on to develop it further in the appropriate way. Because they refuse to exercise such patience, because they instead mark time obstinately at the point where

Marie Bracquemond, *On the Terrace at Sèvres with the Painter Henri Fantin-Latour*, 1880. Oil on canvas, 34¾ x 45¼ in. (88 x 115 cm). Musée du Petit Palais, Geneva, Switzerland.

this development, born of reflexion, ought to begin, these independent artists remain 'Impressionists'" (Thomson).

THE END OF THE STATE-CONTROLLED ART MARKET

During this period, the selection policy operated by the Salon jury was much less restrictive than that of the Impressionists. With almost 7,300 works on show, the Salon of 1880 was the biggest ever, and simply too much to take in; it was also the last to be organized by the State, for in the following year the event became the responsibility of a newly formed artists' grouping, the Société des Artistes Français. Was this the end of State control of the art market? Certainly, the mold had been definitively broken: It had proved impossible to provide a forum for the ever-growing numbers of artists and collectors while simultaneously accommodating the plethora

of styles coexisting independently at any one time. It was not only Zola's "Actualists" who found that the Salon was not helpful; even to conservative artists, the institution that had once set up careers and enhanced sales now mattered less. Artist careers, which in the 1860s were still being made within the context of the Salon, were now played out in a wider field of forces. It was no longer a case of choosing between presence at the Salon and no exhibition at all; quite the contrary: Private galleries and dealers had now cornered the market, leaving official institutions in the shade.

Besides well-known figures of the stature of Paul Durand-Ruel or Georges Petit, more than one hundred art dealers were active in Paris in 1870, and certainly not living exclusively off sales of unknown moderns, for they also represented artists who had already made their name. Auctions like those held since the 1850s by the Hôtel Drouot auction house in Paris were another way to target collectors. However, their effectiveness

Durand-Ruel's invoice relating to sale of pictures by Claude Monet, 1891. Musée Marmottan, Paris.

was hard to predict. An auction of Impressionist works that Renoir arranged in 1875, for example, produced a meager average price of 163 francs per picture.

Of the art dealers, Durand-Ruel was linked longest with the Impressionists. He had initially handled works by Millet and Daubigny and other artists of the Barbizon School, but later, after getting to know Monet and Pissarro in London early in the 1870s, he specialized in Impressionist works. By this time, artworks had become well established as a commodity for speculative trading. Early in 1872, for example, the dealer spent 51,000 francs on a purchase of Manet's.

Renoir's painting *Luncheon of the Boating Party* (ill. p.141) was shown at the seventh Impressionist exhibition and marks the point at which Durand-Ruel embarked on new marketing strategies. He bought the picture after the Paris exhibition ended, and arranged for this large-format canvas to tour the world, putting it on display in Boston, New York, London, and

PAGE 138
Pierre-Auguste Renoir, *Portrait of Paul Durand-Ruel*, 1910.
Oil on canvas, 25½ x 21¼ in. (65 x 54 cm). Private collection, Paris.

PAGE 139
Pierre-Auguste Renoir, *On the Swing*, 1876.
Oil on canvas, 36¼ x 28¾ in. (92 x 73 cm). Musée d'Orsay, Paris.

elsewhere. A collector in Washington, DC, Duncan Phillips, eventually bought it from him in 1923, for $125,000—a sum that ensured it became front-page news. This approach enabled the dealer to have an individual painting generally acknowledged as a masterpiece; and the profit, when it came, was worth the wait.

During the 1880s, Durand-Ruel made repeated efforts to achieve real recognition for the Impressionists beyond the borders of France. As in the early 1870s, he put on exhibitions in London; in Brussels, he showed works by Pissarro, Renoir, Sisley, Monet, Degas, Morisot, and also by Manet and Cassatt, even shipping pictures overseas as far as the United States. Critics and purchasers were not always very impressed. Pissarro received an account from his son Lucien of the 1882–83 London exhibition: "Here the viewers are forced to stand too close to the pictures, and so, as you can imagine, the painting technique causes great consternation" (Rewald). Nor did some of the sales figures give much less cause for consternation, to artists and gallery-owner alike.

Doubtless influenced by the imbroglio surrounding the seventh Impressionist exhibition, as well as by his financial predicament, Durand-Ruel had decided that he would put on single-artist exhibitions. A start was made with an exhibition of the works of Boudin soon after New Year 1883, with Monet, Renoir, and Pissarro following, and then, in June, Sisley. Although sales went well, not all artists were taken with the idea—least of all Gauguin, who felt that what counted was the impact made by the Impressionists collectively, as a group. Degas too, after opting out of the previous year's exhibition, now spoke up, refusing to feature in the current exhibition series.

Concurrently with Durand-Ruel's one-man exhibitions, his greatest competitor, Georges Petit, launched his second "Exposition internationale," a selection of twelve established artists exhibited in sumptuous surroundings. Among those presented were Alexandre Cabanel, Giuseppe de Nittis, and Alfred Stevens. In the mid-1880s, Monet, Renoir, and Sisley began to market their works through Petit as well as through Durand-Ruel, who felt particular resentment in the case of Monet. But the artists took Monet's view that by widening their circle of dealers they could demonstrate to the public at large that their works were not simply the private passion of a single dealer. And Monet, notwithstanding good sales since the 1870s, had no choice but to protect his income, particularly in view of the fact that Durand-Ruel's activities in the United States—where he opened a branch in 1887—were slow to yield worthwhile returns for the painters.

Meanwhile, more and more artists, often with help from critics, were endeavoring to set up exhibitions of their own. One early fruit of the new alliance between artists and art critics was Manet's portrait of Émile Zola (ill. p.54)—one of a whole series of portraits that this artist devoted to his critics. Art connoisseurship rose to new heights of prestige: in many and

Pierre-Auguste Renoir, *Luncheon of the Boating Party*, 1880–81.
Oil on canvas, 51 x 68 in. (129.5 x 172.7 cm).
The Phillips Collection, Washington, DC.

various guises, texts on art found their way into the nineteenth-century daily Press, magazines, and dedicated journals. The boom in print media ran parallel to the diversification of the art market, and the Impressionists turned this to their own advantage: For the first time ever, an art movement made it into the newspaper headlines.

Press coverage expanded with every successive exhibition. From the first exhibition (1874) onward, the Impressionists' advocates—Zola and Castagnary, for example—had always encountered opposition, most prominently from Albert Wolf of *Le Figaro* and Louis Leroy with his satirical essays. Art criticism as such was in its infancy, and major difficulties in writing about the new painting techniques occurred for want of adequate terminology. This can be seen from comparisons of the Impressionist painters with the political Opposition: similarly to the Spanish Anarchists, they were called "Intransigents." The same difficulties, however, might also underlie metaphor-laden critical reviews published by writers who did not even trouble

to distinguish between a painting's subject and its technique. Wolf went on record early on with his proposal that Pissarro should be helped to understand that "the sky is not the color of fresh butter" (cf. p.118).

Théodore Duret, a collector himself, was among the well-disposed critics; by 1878 he had written the first-ever history of Impressionism, and he also put much effort into finding purchasers for Impressionist works. Duret was a close friend of the Charpentiers, a husband and wife who from 1879 onward jointly edited *La Vie Moderne*, an illustrated periodical focused on art and literature. The Charpentiers too were artwork collectors, serious enough to become involved in exhibitions: Manet had shown his work in the setting of their publishing premises, and Monet, Renoir, and Sisley followed suit. Renoir, in particular, had formed close ties with the Charpentier family during the late 1870s, and provided illustrations for a novella that Charpentier proposed to publish. Charpentier's support enabled Renoir to make his home in a small house

Pierre-Auguste Renoir, *Madame Charpentier and her Children*, 1878.
Oil on canvas, 60½ x 75 in. (153.7 x 190.2 cm).
The Metropolitan Museum of Art, New York.

▷ **Édouard Manet**, *At Père Lathuille's*, 1879.
Oil on canvas, 36¼ x 44 in. (92 x 112 cm).
Musée des Beaux-Arts, Tournai, Belgium.

in Montmartre, and it was in the garden here that the famous painting *On the Swing* (ill. p.139) had its genesis, along with other works. Marguerite Charpentier had Renoir paint a portrait of her, together with her daughter Georgette and son Paul, godson to Zola; and she saw to it that the work was there to be admired in the Salon of 1878 (ill. p.142).

Besides the numerous events arranged by gallery owners, art dealers, artists, and collectors, and reviewed at length in the *Press*, there were also various artist groups jostling for a public; the Société Anonyme had led the way. The Union des Femmes Peintres et Sculpteurs, the Cercle de l'Union Artistique, and the Société d'Aquarellistes Français all had annual exhibitions. The Salon des Indépendants was held for the first time in 1884, providing a forum for members of the Société des Artistes Indépendants to exhibit more than 1,000 works representing all schools and styles. Talents as diverse as those of Seurat, Signac,

Redon, van Gogh, and Gauguin contributed to the works on display there; these artists having quit the Société des Artistes Français so that they could hold exhibitions without a jury and without the business of awarding prizes.

From this perspective the Impressionists can be seen as one of many artist groupings seeking to gain a hearing through new tactics, starting with artist colonies like Barbizon or such initiatives as the Salon des Refusés. Eventually, three major annual exhibitions emerged as joint successors to the Salon. The Salon of the Société des Artistes Français was the largest; that of the Société Nationale des Beaux-Arts, founded in 1890 with Meissonier at the helm, was the most exclusive; and the juryless Salon des Indépendants proved to have the greatest stylistic range—and longevity. It has taken place annually, with few interruptions, ever since, and in 2009 will be held for the 120th time.

During the 1880s, the French art scene had its cards reshuffled: a heterogeneous mix of dealers, critics, gallery owners, and private artist groupings took over from the State-controlled Salon. Free enterprise replaced the old institutions. The official Salon had become an anachronism, for the art market had long since become subject to the laws of the free market economy.

MANET'S "DISPENSER OF SOLACE"

The State did in fact present its own successor exhibition to replace the Salon: the Triennale, inaugurated in 1883. However, this venture failed to attract enough interest from the artists. It proved so difficult to fill the walls that in the end virtually every work sent in was hung. At least the venue was big enough, as one critic teased. Once again, a conservatively minded jury was to pronounce its verdict on the exhibits; many of the artists were so certain of being rejected that they did not bother to submit works in the first place. But Fantin-Latour did participate, the German Impressionist Max Liebermann sent a work in, and Auguste Rodin showed, among other things, his first lifesize sculpture, *The Age of Bronze*.

Manet offered five paintings for the Triennale, one of them his young couple painted *en plein air* at the famous Père Lathuille restaurant in Paris (ill. p.143). In this dissimilar pair, not a few contemporary observers saw the protagonists of a liaison that was currently the subject of lively gossip, between the salon beauty Marie Colombier and the writer Paul Bonnetain, who was twenty years her junior. This painting had already provoked controversy at the 1880 Salon. Events the year before had made it impossible to exclude Manet's works

> *"There is only one way to be truthful: at first glance, put down what you see. If it works, it works; if it doesn't, you go back and start again. Anything else is a waste of time."* Édouard Manet

from the exhibition. Following a change in the regulations, he had become one of the artists entitled to deliver their works for exhibition without reference to the jury: he was "hors concours." In late 1881, his old friend Antonin Proust, the new Director of the Beaux-Arts, at last secured for Manet the honor for which the painter had fought so long: He was made a Chevalier de la Légion d'Honneur.

At the Salon in May of the following year, Manet exhibited his famous painting of a theater balcony audience, full house, brightly lit under extravagant chandeliers, watching a trapeze artiste whose legs just protrude into the top left-hand corner of the picture: *A Bar at the Folies Bergères* (ill. pp.144–145). The observer's view of the immediate area in which the dreamy-looking barmaid is standing comes from the reflection in the mirror behind her. But where exactly is the top-hatted gentleman standing in relation to the Parisian "dispenser of solace"? Unlike the barmaid figure, he is visible only in the mirror. The graphic artist Louis Morel-Retz maintained that this was illogical, an "oversight" on the part of the painter. In his caricature of the painting in the *Journal Amusant*, he inserted this figure, seen from the back, into the field of view, adding the note, "A dispenser of solace at the Folies Bergères. (Her back is reflected in the mirror; however, doubtless because of the artist's inattention, a gentleman whose reflection likewise appears in the mirror is nowhere to be seen in the painting. We feel called upon to rectify this omission.)" (Smith). Others considered the painting's composition to indicate that a particular role is assigned to the viewer: He appears in Manet's picture, not entirely flatteringly, as a customer of the "dispenser of solace"—and as a client, for she supplies sexual services as well as alcohol. Echoes of *Nana* and *Olympia* (ill. pp.44–5), indeed. *A Bar at the Folies Bergères* was another of the pictures that the artist submitted for the Triennale, thus declaring himself once again to be a painter of modern life—and one not afraid to pick a fight. Aware since the end of the 1870s that he had syphilis, Manet died on April 30, 1883, at the age of 51, and before the announcement about admission of his works to the Triennale. In fact, all five paintings were rejected.

Édouard Manet, *A Bar at the Folies Bergères*, 1881–82. Oil on canvas, 37¾ x 51¼ in. (96 x 130 cm). The Courtauld Gallery, London.

Alfred Sisley, *On the Banks of the River Loing at Saint-Mammès*, 1885. Oil on canvas, 21½ x 29¼ in. (54.6 x 74 cm). Christie's, London.

▷ Paul Gauguin, *The Farm at La Groue, Osny*, 1883. Oil on canvas, 15 x 18¼ in. (38 x 46.3 cm). Private collection.

"MANET'S GANG" BREAKS UP

The Manet memorial exhibition arranged a year after his death at the École des Beaux-Arts drew big crowds, and the level of interest still remained high at the subsequent auction of his works. Manet had directed in his will that this event was to be managed by Théodore Duret. For a while longer, "Manet's Gang"—as the Impressionist painters had been dubbed a decade earlier—continued to meet for "dîners" together; Morisot, as a woman, could not attend, but instead hosted memorial gatherings at her home. However, interest in such meetings waned, and over time the artists met less and less often, whether in Paris or for shared painting sojourns out of town; no plans were made to hold further exhibitions as a group. Sisley—seldom in Paris and a long way away from the artistic milieu—picked up again on his earlier works, both thematically and stylistically. He moved base several times between various villages north and west of Paris, including Argenteuil, Louveciennes, and Bougival, and painted these

areas of the Île-de-France; his interest in the light effects observed in snow-covered landscapes, a subject that had absorbed many of the Impressionists during the 1870s, endured to the end of his life (ill. p.149). He painted the riverbanks at Saint-Mammès over and over again, at the confluence of the Seine and the Loing, varying his standpoints and sometimes integrating the railroad bridge over the Loing into his composition (ill. p.146). Vigorous brushstrokes delineate plants and the water surface, showing how Sisley developed technically over these years, whereas the sky is more reminiscent of the layered application of paint of his earlier works (cf. ill. pp.100–01). In 1889, with his wife and two children, the painter settled in Moret-sur-Loing, to the south of the capital, on the fringe of the Forest of Fontainebleau. He described his surroundings there to Monet as "not a bad part of the world, rather a chocolate-box landscape" (*Französische Meisterwerke*).

Cézanne continued to paint in his native Provence; Pissarro had ended up in 1884 at Eragny, near Pontoise, France. Caillebotte

spent much of his time in Petit Gennevilliers, across the Seine from Argenteuil, still engrossed in his painting and producing landscapes, portraits, and still lifes (ill. p.166). Gauguin moved to Copenhagen in 1884 to try his luck, his Danish wife having already moved back there. But he fell victim there to a number of unscrupulous tricks, and returned to Paris the following summer (ill. p.147).

Claude Monet settled in 1883 in Giverny, where he could give free rein to his love of gardening, and here, over the next four decades, he created his own world of subjects to paint. His two sons made the move too, as did the Hoschedé family: Five years back, when both had been in deep water financially, the painter and the collector had made common cause. In these years Monet developed into the best business brain among the Impressionist painters. He had been quick to approach the art dealer Georges Petit as an alternative to Durand-Ruel. Early

in 1888, Monet agreed with Theo van Gogh—brother of the painter Vincent van Gogh—to hold a first exhibition. It was to be at the Boussod and Valadon gallery, located on the Boulevard Montmartre and run by Theo van Gogh. Monet obtained good terms: he received 1,200 francs for each of a total of ten works, and even took a cut when they were sold. In February 1889, Theo van Gogh arranged another exhibition for him, this time in London; in the fall of that year the dealer negotiated the impressive price of 10,000 francs for a Monet work. And in 1889, too, finally, the painter was accorded a major retrospective at Petit's, shared with the sculptor Auguste Rodin.

Renoir remained faithful to the Salon after the artists took over, exhibiting there for the last time as late as 1890. He also maintained links with Durand-Ruel, the art dealer, always updating him on his progress. During the 1880s Renoir was fascinated in particular by the works of the Old Masters,

Claude Monet, *Gale on the Belle-Île Coast*, 1886.
Oil on canvas, 25½ x 32 in. (65 x 81.5 cm). Musée d'Orsay, Paris.

▽ **Paul Signac**, *Snow, Butte Montmartre*, 1887.
 Oil on canvas, 6¼ x 9½ in. (15.8 x 24 cm). Private collection.

Alfred Sisley, *Snow at Louveciennes*, 1878.
Oil on canvas, 24 x 20 in. (61 x 50.5 cm). Musée d'Orsay, Paris.

Neither sub-zero temperatures nor howling gales nor anything else, it seemed, could deter the Impressionists from painting outdoors. The lighting effects that came about after a snowfall were a subject of particular fascination for many of them. Monet even wrested a number of works from the harsh climate of Brittany, France, expressing himself in euphoric terms to the art dealer Durand-Ruel, "The sea is unbelievably beautiful and accompanied by fantastic rock formations, and incidentally this place is called 'The Savage Sea'...I love this mysterious region, above all because it is forcing me to venture out beyond the things I normally do. I have to confess that I am having great difficulty in capturing this gloomy and terrible aspect."

Pierre-Auguste Renoir, *Venice, Grand Canal*, 1881.
Oil on canvas, 21¼ x 25½ in. (54 x 65.1 cm).
Museum of Fine Arts, Boston, MA, U.S., Bequest of Alexander Cochrane.

Renoir's view of the best-known waterway in Venice has one quality
above all else: It is flooded with light. Reflected on the water, the canal
front *palazzi* and the cloud-flecked sky shimmer in multicolored light.
Even the dark gondolas show no trace of black: Renoir chose instead
to put them on his canvas in a subdued glow of wine-red and bluish
tones. Durand-Ruel liked this painting: The artist was scarcely back
from his Italian journey when his dealer showed it at the seventh
Impressionist exhibition, in 1882.

PAGE 152
Pierre-Auguste Renoir, *Dancing in the City*, 1882–83.
Oil on canvas, 70¾ x 35½ in. (180 x 90 cm). Musée d'Orsay, Paris.

PAGE 153
Pierre-Auguste Renoir, *Umbrellas*, ca. 1881–86. Oil on canvas,
70¾ x 45¼ in. (180 x 115 cm). The National Gallery, London.

Pierre-Auguste Renoir, *Sketch for The Bathers*, ca. 1884–85. Red chalk and pastel on paper, 42½ x 63¾ in. (108 x 162 cm). Musée d'Orsay, Paris.

together with the subjects provided by the modern metropolis. He loved the Louvre's collections, taking a special interest in French Rococo painting (ill. p.152). In 1881, forty years old and already an established artist, he undertook his Grand Tour to Italy, visiting Venice, Rome, and Palermo, while taking time to study Italian art (ill. pp.150–51). He stayed a particularly long time at Naples, but was dissatisfied with the progress he made there, as he wrote to Durand-Ruel in November of that year: "I regret to say I am still experimenting, feeling unsatisfied and wiping everything off, time after time. Hopefully this mania will pass off soon...I am behaving like a child at school. A clean white sheet waiting for some neat handwriting, and then splosh—an ink blot. I am still spraying blots around and I am forty years old" (Rewald).

Renoir's painting *Umbrellas* (ill. p.153) could almost serve as an illustration of those words to Durand-Ruel. On a busy street, pedestrians are jostling in the rain. A small girl is looking directly at the observer, but his eye is caught by the simply dressed woman with no umbrella. In the prominent center of the painting, only hands and umbrellas are to be seen; some of the figures are sliced across by the edge of the picture. Through careful composition, Renoir has produced

the suggestion of a snapshot, very much in the Impressionist tradition (cf. ill. pp.94–5). In terms of technique too, the painter has returned to the sketch-style strokes and dabs with the brush that characterized many of his earlier works. However, the red-headed woman on the left-hand side of the picture is distinctly different from the rest of the figures shown. After returning from Italy, Renoir reworked this female figure: the colors of her clothing became duller; the figure looks more three-dimensional, and is thrown into relief in comparison with the rather perfunctorily treated background by its contours and its smoother surface. The dress was designed by the artist to conform to the current fashion, and that in turn provides the basis for dating the changes to about 1885.

Renoir continued to travel and to experiment; he stopped painting outdoors, and in his studio returned to focusing more on drawing. Working from reliefs by the French sculptor François Girardon (1628–1715), and producing a large number of sketches on the way, he was preparing a composition that was to keep him occupied for three years: women bathing in a river (ill. pp.154–5). In 1887, the artist showed his *Bathers* at Petit's gallery. Renoir's control of line found some admirers, but scarcely any of his Impressionist comrades felt able to share his

Pierre-Auguste Renoir, *The Bathers*, 1884–87. Oil on canvas,
45½ x 67 in. (115.6 x 170 cm). Philadelphia Museum of Art, PA, U.S.

enthusiasm for the artists of the seventeenth and eighteenth centuries, or to follow his return to a smooth painting style. In retrospect, the Impressionist works he produced during the 1870s, while he was collaborating closely with Monet, are perhaps best regarded as representing one of many different painterly styles and techniques practiced by Renoir, in some cases concurrently. In his view, the decorative character with which he endowed his later works carried no negative associations: "There are enough ugly things around in life and there is no need to add more," commented the author of almost 6,000 creative works (*Französische Meisterwerke*). In his subjects too, Renoir was not circumscribed. For a long period he earned his living as a portraitist, a type of work apt to entail appreciable stylistic concessions to meet clients' requirements.

Neither Renoir nor Monet nor Sisley could be tempted to contribute to a future Impressionist exhibition, for which, after a four-year gap, plans were beginning to crystallize. Once again, disagreements arose over the issue of participation by Degas and his circle. However, this time Pissarro too had clear priorities, contending strongly that Georges Seurat and Paul Signac should be included. Gauguin, unhappy about the break-up of the group, which he thought Durand-Ruel

was encouraging, identified himself with Pissarro's view, but found no further support. Morisot and her husband eventually managed to reconcile almost all the interested parties, and only Caillebotte declined to take part. The difficulty of establishing a common denominator for works by the exhibiting artists was further demonstrated by the title chosen for the show, which was held in Rue Laffitte and opened its doors on May 15, 1886, as, baldly, the "Eighth Exhibition of Paintings." This time the participating artists did not want to be designated "independent artists," for fear of confusion with the "Indépendants," who had been holding a yearly Salon since 1884. Berthe Morisot contributed (ill. pp.158–9); the works contributed by Gauguin and Guillaumin, like Morisot's, were in the Impressionist manner. Mary Cassatt and Marie Bracquemond also contributed, and Degas' friend, Forain, was likewise represented once more. Pissarro, Seurat, and Signac were given a room to themselves, in which Seurat had space to hang his monumental canvas *A Sunday Afternoon on the Island of La Grande Jatte*, and it was here too that Lucien Pissarro, Camille's eldest son, was able to show his debut paintings.

Degas caused a stir at this eighth Impressionist exhibition with a series of nudes in pastel. For years past he had been

Edgar Degas, *Dancer at the Barre*, ca. 1885.
Charcoal with pastel and chalk on paper, 12¼ x 9¼ in. (31.1 x 23.5 cm).
Fred Jones Jr. Museum of Art, The University of Oklahoma, U.S.,
Norman, Aaron M. and Clara Weitzenhoffer Bequest, 2000.

Edgar Degas, *Standing Nude*, ca. 1886.
Pastel on paper, 26¼ x 20½ in. (67 x 52 cm). Private collection.

Edgar Degas, *Woman in Bathtub Washing her Leg*, 1878.
Pastel on paper, 7¾ x 16¼ in. (19.7 x 41 cm). Musée d'Orsay, Paris.

▷ Edgar Degas, *The Star* or *Dancer on Stage*, ca. 1876–77.
Pastel on paper, 23½ x 17¼ in. (60 x 44 cm). Musée d'Orsay, Paris.

Berthe Morisot, *Young Woman at Needlework in the Garden*, 1884.
Oil on canvas, 23¼ x 28¼ in. (59 x 72 cm).
National Gallery of Scotland, Edinburgh.

working on a variety of techniques and formats. He valued pastels for their matte surfaces (ill. pp.156–7), and for the same reason used them to prime his canvases. In the work he showed in 1886, Degas had concentrated on female nudes, which he studied in the acts of bathing, washing, toweling themselves, and combing their hair.

The artist remained faithful to his preference for surprising perspectives, this time positioning the observer close up to the figures, who for their part are completely self-absorbed. Degas shunned artificial poses, letting the women follow natural movements—appearing so natural that the critic Gustave Geffroy surmised the artist was observing his models through the keyhole. Later reviewers, less cautious in their choice of words, considered the works and the painter to be both arrogant and misogynist—a criticism that was to persist

for a long time, in spite of the many voices supporting Degas. One reason for this was the use of quotations, or of remarks maliciously attributed to the artist, such as the comment that his nudes showed "human creatures occupied with their own person—cats licking themselves." In this context, further room for speculation was generated by the artist's long bachelorhood: He was the only Impressionist painter to remain unmarried, although this did not prevent him from confronting the art dealer Ambroise Vollard with a surprising insight, "Vollard, people need to get married." "Why don't you get married, then?" "Oh, I didn't mean getting married myself, of course. I would be much too afraid of my wife looking at a finished picture and telling me it was really quite nice" (Krems). After the 1886 exhibition, Degas stopped showing his works in public, apart from a one-man exhibition featuring landscapes at Durand-

Berthe Morisot, *Girl in the Garden*, 1885.
Oil on canvas, 24¼ x 29¾ in. (61.3 x 75.6 cm).
The Museum of Fine Arts, Houston, TX, U.S., Gift of Audrey Jones Beck.

Ruel's gallery in 1892. In any case, Degas sold his works only when he needed cash.

Some of the reviews of the 1886 exhibition hovered around the topic of Degas and his nudes; however, the main focus of attention proved to be the works of the newly admitted artists, Seurat and Signac. Félix Fénéon, a journalist and art critic, devoted a series of articles to this exhibition. The absence of such earlier protagonists as Renoir, Monet, Cézanne, and Sisley certainly made a major difference, he felt. Yet, "even with these gaps, the new exhibition is highly illuminating: Degas, who loathes being described as an Impressionist, is there with some characteristic works; Mme. Morisot, Gauguin, and Guillaumin represent Impressionism as seen in earlier exhibitions; Pissarro, Seurat, and Signac are the innovators" (Rewald). Not all reviewers found the position to be so

clear, and even among the other exhibitors enthusiasm was decidedly restrained, not least because from their point of view the show was being stolen by the "innovators." Degas referred drily to Seurat as a "notary"; for Gauguin, he was the "chemist."

GEORGES SEURAT

Georges Seurat, a Parisian by birth, had been studying at the École des Beaux-Arts for a year when he went to see the fourth Impressionist exhibition. That same year, at the age of nineteen, he left the academy. He taught himself the Impressionist style of painting, taking up their way of applying short discrete dabs with the brush and using unmixed pigments (ill. p.160).

Georges Seurat, *The Circus*, 1891.
Oil on canvas, 73 x 60 in. (185.5 x 152.5 cm). Musée d'Orsay, Paris.

◁ **Georges Seurat**, *Rue Saint-Vincent, Montmartre, in Spring*, ca. 1884.
Oil on wood, 9¾ x 6 in. (24.8 x 15.4 cm).
The Fitzwilliam Museum, Cambridge, England.

PAGES 162–3
Georges Seurat, *A Sunday Afternoon on the Island of La Grande Jatte*,
1884–86. Oil on canvas, 81¾ x 121¼ in. (207.5 x 308.1 cm).
The Art Institute of Chicago, IL, U.S.

Georges Seurat, *Bathers at Asnières*, 1883–84. Oil on canvas,
79¼ x 118 in. (201 x 300 cm). The National Gallery, London.

▷ Paul Signac, *The Bridge at Asnières*, 1888.
Oil on canvas, 18 x 25½ in. (46 x 65 cm). Private collection.

His interest extended beyond painting to the science of optics. Seurat embraced theories of color, studied the works of Delacroix, and learned from material published by scientists, including the chemist Eugène Chevreul and the physicist and painter Ogden N. Rood, that the perception of mixed colors actually occurs "in the eye itself" (see Feature, pp.78–9).

Having drawn his conclusions from these studies, he reduced his palette to the four primary colors and their intermediate shades, arranging them on the palette in spectrum order: blue, blue-violet, violet, violet-red, red, and so on. Seurat did not mix his pigments at all, with the result that when seen close up his works positively flicker and shimmer. Seen from further away, the Pointillist technique supports the impression of flat brushwork.

At the first exhibition held by the Société des Artistes Indépendants, which he had cofounded, Seurat presented the fruits of his approach for the first time, in the unglamorous surroundings of the canteen serving the exhibition premises. The critics were divided over his 6½- by 10-foot (2-meter by 3-meter) canvas *Bathers at Asnières* (ill. p.164), for which he had made numerous chalk and oil studies. In terms of subject matter he was close to the Impressionists. Asnières, one of the Seine

villages to the west of Paris, was a resort for the leisure pursuits of the city-dwellers, with an industrial backdrop, it is true; but then Sisley and Manet too sometimes incorporated chimney stacks and railroad bridges into their views of Argenteuil and its surroundings (cf. ill. pp.118–19, 146). While Seurat's technique of short, successively superimposed brushstrokes and dabs is reminiscent of Impressionist paintings, it nonetheless made a considerable impact because of the great luminosity of the painting's surface. There was nothing arbitrary about how Seurat juxtaposed his colors, for he based his approach on complementary color contrasts, with a view to making them as luminous as possible.

In the same year, 1884, Seurat started work on a new composition of equally monumental proportions. During the first few months he made more than sixty sketches of the trippers on the Seine island of La Grande Jatte, not far from Asnières. However, his painting *A Sunday Afternoon on the Island of La Grande Jatte* (ill. pp.162–3) was composed in the studio, *plein-air* work being inappropriate for his intricate composition and effortful style of painting. The painting was completed (for the moment) in March 1885; large numbers of visitors were shown assembled in their Sunday best—sitting, standing, skipping,

and rowing small boats. During that summer Seurat decided to rework the picture, covering the original paint layer with thousands of colored flecks.

This, then, was the work that Seurat presented at the eighth Impressionist exhibition, in spring 1886. The Impressionists' practice of breaking away from object colors was taken a stage further by Seurat: The "points" that he distributes, mosaic-fashion, over the canvas are brought together only in the eye of the beholder to form a motif—color and motif being in reality far apart. Seurat persuaded several fellow-painters to share his enthusiasm for this Pointillist technique; one of them was Paul Signac, whom he had first met at the Salon des Indépendants in 1884 (ill. pp.148, 165).

Vincent van Gogh saw Neo-Impressionist works in the shop run by his Paris paints merchant, Père Tanguy (ill. p.70). The Dutchman and Signac became friends; they would often take painting trips to the outer suburbs of Paris, and from time to time van Gogh tried his hand at "Pointillisme," as the less enthusiastic critics called it at the time. Both Pissarro and his son Lucien proved capable of achieving fine results with Seurat's laborious technique. Often accused of failing to finish

his works adequately, Pissarro senior had been having doubts with regard to his Impressionist style. Like Renoir, he had rediscovered drawing, and from the beginning of the 1880s had concentrated on figure painting (ill. p.167). Later, Pissarro embraced Seurat's method; his small-format *Woman in the Field, Springtime Sun at Eragny* (ill. p.166) shows his adoption of Pointillist ways. At the final Impressionist exhibition, thanks to Fénéon, the painting style of Seurat and his adherents acquired a name of its own: Neo-Impressionism. Seurat himself preferred the term "Divisionism" for his method of painting, as this aptly referred to the technique's prismatic separation of colors.

For Fénéon, by 1887, the position was quite clear, and so he could view it with a touch of irony: "The heyday of Impressionism has passed. Back then, the unconstrained public rocked with laughter at the sight of the white frames round the Impressionist pictures, recommended that these crazy folk should be taken off for psychiatric attention, pitied their color-blindness, jeered and whistled at them as clowns. But today the visitors look, partly understanding what they see, and if they still grin, it is not without some embarrassment" (*Impressionist Masterpieces*).

Camille Pissarro, *Woman in the Field, Springtime Sun at Eragny*, 1887.
Oil on canvas, 21½ x 25½ in. (54.5 x 65 cm). Musée d'Orsay, Paris.

Gustave Caillebotte, *Still Life with Melon and Bowl of Figs*, 1880–82.
Oil on canvas, 21¼ x 25½ in. (54 x 65 cm).
Private collection.

Camille Pissarro, *View of the Prison at Pontoise*, 1881.
Oil on canvas, 23½ x 29¼ in. (60 x 74 cm). Private collection.

Camille Pissarro, *Père Melon Sawing
Logs, Pontoise*, 1879.
Oil on canvas, 35 x 45¾ in.
(89 x 116.2 cm). Private collection.

SERIES PICTURES AND THE POST-IMPRESSIONISTS

LA MARE DE BELLE-CROIX.

— Sapristi ! un peintre dans l'eau !...
— Oh ! nous avons beaucoup d'Anglais et d'Américains en ce moment dans la forêt; ils cherchent tous à faire leurs études à des places où personne ne s'est mis avant eux...

This cartoon mocking *plein-air* painters appeared on September 18, 1875 in *Le Journal Amusant*. Bibliothèque Nationale, Paris.

The two gentleman at back left are profoundly astonished by what they see occupying the "Faircross Pool":
—Goodness gracious! There's a painter in the pond!...
—Well, you see, there are currently large numbers of English and American people here in the forest; they are all eager to do their studies in some place where nobody has tried it before...

The year 1894 marked the death of a man who had collected Impressionist works since the very beginning: Gustave Caillebotte. He bequeathed his art treasures to the French State. But the beneficiary's delight at this rich harvest of artworks—it included Manet's *The Balcony* (ill. p.63), Sisley's *Regatta at Molesey* (ill. pp.100–101), Degas' *The Star* (ill. p.157), and Renoir's *On the Swing* (ill. p.139)—was decidedly muted. Salon painters and Academy professors even feared for France's honor, were Caillebotte's gift, which they regarded as "garbage," to be exhibited in public. Renoir, who had the thankless role of executor, spent two years wrangling with the French authorities. By 1896, while he had not actually brought the opponents round to his point of view, their resistance was at least beginning to crumble. The State now agreed to accept

Caillebotte's bequest, comprising forty works by installments, and thus ensured possession of the core holdings of the Musée d'Orsay, inaugurated ninety years later.

From the date of the negotiations over the Caillebotte collection, which, from today's perspective, verge on the absurd, it took barely thirty years for the tide to turn completely. The French State had come to realize the immense art-historical importance of the pictures concerned, and an offer was made to accept the hitherto rejected part of the collection after all— only to be politely refused by the Caillebotte heirs. Reluctantly, the State followed where the private collectors had led. The first Berthe Morisot had been acquired for the nation in 1894, the first Monet in 1907—a view of Rouen Cathedral—and ten years later still came the first purchase of a Degas, this from the studio sales following the artist's death. Cézanne, however, could be said to have had no reversal of fortune following his run of failures at the Salons: Not one of his pictures was acquired by the State museums during his lifetime.

The tardiness of the official blessing is all the more astonishing in the light of the evolution in artistic taste that was already becoming perceptible as far back as the 1880s. At the fifth Paris World's Fair in 1900, the works of Impressionist painters were at last given a room of their own within the fine arts exhibition. With this popularization of Impressionist painting techniques and motifs, however, something was lost: The capacity to provoke that had once been inherent in many Impressionist works now vanished almost without trace. Even Academy painters went over to the sketching style of painting and the bright palette for their works; *plein-air* painting had in any case been well established long ago. Degas, living quietly in Paris, was appalled at the success now attending the Salon artists, who were celebrating easy triumphs along a road made level for them by the Impressionists: "They call us names, while rifling our pockets" (*Impressionist Masterpieces*).

▷ **Claude Monet**, *The Portal, Harmony in Blue*, 1893.
Oil on canvas, 35¾ x 24¾ in. (91 x 63 cm).
Musée d'Orsay, Paris.

PAGES 168–9
Claude Monet, *Waterlilies* (detail), 1908.
Oil on canvas, 36¼ x 35 in. (92 x 89 cm). Private collection.

Alfred Sisley, *Lady's Cove, Wales*, 1897. Oil on canvas,
18 x 24 in. (46 x 61 cm). Musée des Beaux-Arts, Rouen, France.

▷ **Camille Pissarro**, *Rouen Harbour, Quai Saint-Sever*, 1896.
Oil on canvas, 14 x 18 in. (35.5 x 45.7 cm). Christie's, New York.

The art dealers of Paris recorded growing demand for Impressionist works, a trend to which Degas alone was an exception. Durand-Ruel only succeeded once more, in 1892, in interesting Degas in holding a single-artist exhibition of his landscapes. Many of his pastels, and more particularly his works sculpted in wax, never even left his studio. At his death in 1917 about 150 sculpted works were still there. Degas was convinced that posterity would never see these racehorses and girl dancers in wax, clay, cork, or plasticine; but in that he was quite wrong, and before long about half of them had been given permanence in bronze. He had said, "My sculptures are never going to convey that sense of finishedness which is the 'ne plus ultra' of the sculptor; because obviously no one is going to see these experiments…before I die, they will have fallen apart of their own accord" (Smith).

When Ambroise Vollard recalled his early days as an art dealer, he would wax euphoric, "Eighteen ninety! What a wonderful time that was to be an art collector! Masterpieces wherever you looked—and for peanuts" (Vollard). However, Monet in particular and a number of his fellow artists were by then no longer obliged to sell off their works "for peanuts," and could live and work in comfortable circumstances.

Alfred Sisley was the only painter whose works did not appreciate significantly during his lifetime—not even his *Lady's Cove, Wales* of 1897 (ill. p.172). Living out of the swim at Moret-sur-Loing, Sisley had few periods free of financial hardship, and this was in spite of his good contacts with dealers and major collectors. It was not until the year after his death that the prices fetched by his works rose considerably. This was the fate that befell Berthe Morisot too; but at the beginning of the 1890s she had managed to land several important exhibitions. Durand-Ruel, Petit, and Boussod and Valadon exhibited her paintings. In 1894, she received recognition from a surely unexpected quarter. A year before her death—she was to die at the age of fifty-four from complications following influenza—her *Young Woman in Ball Gown* of 1876 was acquired by the French State for 4,500 francs.

Sisley in the end parted company with Durand-Ruel, exhibiting thereafter only under Petit's aegis, but Camille Pissarro kept faith with the dealer who had been there at the start, had put on a major exhibition for him in 1892, and even subsidized his travel.

Pissarro undertook journeys to London and Rouen to paint; the Normandy seaport in particular proved congenial for him, and a first visit in 1883 was followed by others in 1896 and 1898 (ill. p.173). By then his enthusiasm for Pointillism was waning, and he actually overpainted some of his canvases from that phase, returning to his Impressionist technique, as, for example, in his views of Paris boulevards (ill. p.85). These paintings in particular proved very marketable; but that certainly did not mean there could be an unruffled artist–dealer relationship. In 1896, Pissarro complained to his son Lucien that, "Durand is recommending me to paint sunny pictures, bright, luminous ones, the kind the market wants" (Smith).

Renoir would need no prompting to keep the dealer up to date with what was happening. By the end of the 1880s, after years of experimentation with clear drawing and modeling, he saw his way forward once more: "I have gone back to my old soft style of painting, with a light brush, and I shall not give it up again" (*Französische Meisterwerke*, ill. pp.174–5).

Durand-Ruel, to whom these words were addressed, was presumably quite happy about their message, as he arranged a major exhibition for Renoir in 1892. At almost fifty years of age, Renoir had also been sure enough of the woman at his side to get married to her in 1890, by which time their son Pierre was five years old. Aline Charigot had modeled for Renoir on several occasions, among them the time she had modeled the lady with the dog in *Luncheon of the Boating Party* (ill. p.141); nevertheless, he kept the relationship secret, and Morisot was astounded when she finally met Renoir's family in 1891. When the painter finally settled on the Côte d'Azur, at Cagnes, it was

◁ **Pierre-Auguste Renoir,** *Two Girls at the Piano*, 1892.
Oil on canvas, 45¾ x 35½ in. (116 x 90 cm). Musée d'Orsay, Paris.

Pierre-Auguste Renoir, *Nude Figure Seen from behind*, ca. 1909.
Oil on canvas, 16¼ x 20½ in. (41 x 52 cm). Musée d'Orsay, Paris.

not only his wife and three children that he gathered round him: a number of other artists followed him there, one of them Pierre Bonnard.

MONET'S SERIES PAINTINGS

Claude Monet was still interested in natural light effects, on which he was already working concentratedly in the 1880s, producing series pictures. He visited Normandy repeatedly, staying for several months at a time, and finding that its dramatic coastlines presented him with a wealth of challenging subjects. The writer Guy de Maupassant watched Monet painting on the beach there, noting with astonishment that the painter never worked on one canvas for more than a few minutes at a time, but always stopped when the natural light

changed. In 1886, Maupassant recorded that Monet always had children round him as he painted, "holding five or six pictures for him that showed the same subject at different times of day and with different effects. He would reach for one picture at a time and later put it aside, depending on how the sky changed" (*Französische Meisterwerke*).

Having first worked on picture series while staying at Étretat, Monet continued over the following decades to pursue the same interest intensively in Rouen, Venice, and London. He probably gained additional motivation from the resounding financial success of his first series exhibition, which was held at Durand-Ruel's gallery in 1891. He would observe the subtlest nuances of light and atmosphere, so subtle that even the artist did not really capture them until work was well under way. The main actors in a total of twenty-five works, and among the best-known and most hackneyed motifs in Monet's œuvre,

Jean-François Millet, *The Haystacks, Autumn*, ca. 1874.
Oil on canvas, 33½ x 43½ in. (85.1 x 110.2 cm).
The Metropolitan Museum of Art, New York.

were haystacks and ricks. This simple theme had enthused Millet, whose pictures Monet had admired during a large-scale retrospective in Paris in 1887 (ill. p.176). Monet tells us about his progress with this motif, to which he returned in 1888: "When I started I was like the others, because I imagined that two canvases, one for dull weather and one for sunshine, would be enough; but hardly had I started to capture this sunny moment when just a little later the light conditions would have changed already, so that two canvases were not sufficient to capture a faithful impression of this specific aspect of nature, as opposed to a picture compiled from a number of different impressions" (Arnold, ill. p.177).

In Rouen, in 1892, Monet rented a room for himself directly opposite the west façade of the cathedral, devoting more than twenty paintings to this subject (ill. p.171). The pictures of the Houses of Parliament in London and of the Thames bridges that he began while in the British capital in 1899 came back to

France with him, where he worked on them in his studio until 1903. As Durand-Ruel was subsidizing Monet's painting travels, he had to be put aside by the artist during this period. Monet wrote, "I am unable to send you even a single London picture, because it is essential for me to have them all here in front of me, and to be quite honest with you, not one of them is finally finished. I shall finish them all simultaneously" (*Französische Meisterwerke*). In May of the following year, the dealer's patience was rewarded: He now had thirty-seven London scenes by Monet to present to the public (ill. p.191).

PAGE 177, ABOVE
Claude Monet, *Haystacks at Sunset in Winter*, 1891.
Oil on canvas, 25½ x 36¼ in. (65 x 92 cm). Private collection.

PAGE 177, BELOW
Claude Monet, *The "Demoiselles" of Giverny*, 1894.
Oil on canvas, 25½ x 39¼ in. (65 x 100 cm). Private collection.

"And art such as Monet's, the art of the Impressionist, aspiring to capture the essence of a fleeting moment and the subtlest nuances of color, demands supreme mastery of form. Just as the piano virtuoso's fingertips contain all the notes, so the Impressionist artist must have control over forms."

Andreas Aubert, Norwegian art critic, 1883

The Grand Canal (ill. pp.178–9) and the Seine too were further subjects that Monet found congenial. His home at Giverny likewise gave Monet enough material for pictures forming a series; between 1913 and 1926 he immortalized the waterlilies in his garden pond in over 120 variants (ill. pp.180–81).

As far back as 1881, Gauguin had told Pissarro of his concern that repeated treatments of a subject at Durand-Ruel's request were becoming excessive in the cases of Sisley and Monet. He felt that the market was becoming flooded, and that the countless pictures of rowboats and views of Chatou would become a "dreadful trademark" attached to Durand-Ruel. A former stockbroker himself, Gauguin was both a collector and a speculator in the art field, and it may be that his concerns over the picture series were in part rooted in his own collecting interests. However, selling the pictures proved not to be a problem. Durand-Ruel had already shown himself to be an innovative dealer not at all averse to risk, and had little difficulty in successfully placing Monet's series on the art market. While it was not uncommon for contemporaries, fellow painters in particular, to react with bafflement or distaste, the serial way of working seemed to appeal to the public's taste; indeed, to judge by current prices at auction, this is still true today (see Feature, pp.190–91). After Monet died in 1926, certainly, the enthusiasm over his *Waterlilies* fell away to some extent, but its modernity was recognized after the end of World War II, particularly by the American Expressionists. They fêted Monet's late works as installations, "all-over" compositions—lacking a principal subject, but covering the entire canvas. Ellsworth Kelly, recalling his first visit to the painter's studio at Giverny, wrote,

Claude Monet, *The Doge's Palace, Venice*, 1908.
Oil on canvas, 32 x 39 in. (81.3 x 99.1 cm).
Brooklyn Museum, New York, Gift of A. Augustus Healy.

Claude Monet, *Waterlilies*, 1908.
Oil on canvas, 36¼ x 35 in. (92 x 89 cm). Private collection.

▷ **Claude Monet,** *The House Seen from the Rose Garden*, 1922–24.
Oil on canvas, 35 x 39¼ in. (89 x 100 cm). Musée Marmottan, Paris.

Over a period of more than thirty years, Claude Monet constructed a literally inexhaustible source of inspiration for himself: Behind his home at Giverny, little by little, the painter created a garden paradise that he eventually came to regard as one of his works, and indeed "one of the most beautiful" of those. In the early years it was most often the ever-changing colors of the flower-garden's profusion of varieties that he evoked on his canvases, but his last years were devoted almost exclusively to the lilies of his "water garden."

In Monet's late works, the observer often looks in vain for some perspective that will convey structure, or for any points fixed in space, or stabilizing lines. This detachment from the factual world in favor of pure color is what enabled the Impressionist movement's cofounder to become also the artist who transcended Impressionism, and thus points far into a future in which artists like Jackson Pollock or Jean-Paul Riopelle were to find the great Frenchman furnishing key impulses for their own creativity.

"I was impressed. I had never seen pictures like these: all-over compositions with impasto textures, depicting waterlilies, with no horizon... . Monet's late pictures had a lot of influence on me. Even though my work is not comparable with them, I feel I have a related mental attitude" (Dippel).

THE POST-IMPRESSIONISTS

While Monet went on after his final showing in an Impressionist exhibition to plunge enthusiastically into the art of reproducing light and color, and sought to reproduce his visual perceptions naturalistically, other painters had their doubts about Impressionism. Pissarro felt the lack of a well-founded method, on occasion taking the view that the Pointillists had what he sought; Renoir thought his technique required to be further worked on; Cézanne abandoned the spontaneous, sketch-type approach to painting. The Neo-Impressionists had committed themselves to analysis of color; others were less interested in the effects of light than in a work's symbolic import and abstract qualities.

Another seeker after new approaches in art was Paul Gauguin, who had allied himself with the Impressionists in 1879. Having lost his job as a stockbroker in the market crash of 1882, he concentrated solely on painting—only to find that among the Independent or Impressionist artists any group-generated dynamism that might have existed was smothered under individual searching, a situation exacerbated, in Gauguin's view, by Durand-Ruel. The outcome of the final

Paul Gauguin, *Landscape at Pont-Aven*, 1886.
Oil on canvas, 23½ x 28¾ in. (60 x 73 cm). Private collection.

Impressionist exhibition in particular left Gauguin dissatisfied, to put it mildly. In this exhibition, Seurat had played the principal role, and Gauguin's relations with Seurat were not good. He was at loggerheads with Cézanne too, but found Cézanne's painting style so fascinating that he bought pictures from him and mistrustfully scrutinized every step in his artistic progress: "Has Cézanne found the precise, universally valid formula? Should he discover the recipe, the secret of concentrating the condensed expression of all his perceptions into one specific mode, then I beg you to administer to him one of those mysterious homeopathic preparations that will enable you to interrogate him in his sleep, and then to make all haste to Paris and inform us." This was Gauguin's request to his own and Cézanne's mutual friend Pissarro (Thomson). But he became increasingly estranged from the latter also, as Pissarro shared the Anarchist convictions that were taking root

in the weak Third Republic, and in common with several Neo-Impressionists was calling for an egalitarian social order.

And Gauguin himself? He took his leave of the Paris art scene and moved to Brittany, which had retained its peasant-life traditions because of its distance from the center. Once there, he occupied himself initially with landscape work (ill. p.182); then, during his second stay, he turned his attention to Breton ways and customs. A large number of painters had settled in Pont-Aven, a village near the westernmost tip of Brittany. Gauguin was already a well-known name there, and he was happy to offer useful tips to help fellow painters along, including the advice not to paint too much after nature: "The work of art is an abstraction," he informed one of the painters, Émile Schuffenecker (Thomson).

Some of Gauguin's pictures from this period still show the short horizontal brushstrokes of his impressionistic

Paul Gauguin, *The Arlésiennes (Mistral)*, 1888. Oil on canvas,
28¾ x 36¼ in. (73 x 92 cm). The Art Institute of Chicago, IL, U.S.,
Mr. and Mrs. Lewis Larned Coburn Memorial Collection.

period, even though he had already abandoned his realistic or naturalistic style of that time. Gauguin now simplified both coloration and draftsmanship; convinced that the key point was the picture's symbolic import, he turned to clear outlines, geometrized forms, and uniform color areas.

The new clarity of outline, reminiscent of Japanese woodcuts, led critics to talk of a "cloisonné" technique (Fr. *cloisonner*, to subdivide, separate). In his *The Arlésiennes (Mistral)* (ill. p.183), painted during his brief period living with Vincent van Gogh in Provence, Gauguin dispensed with a horizon. Elements in the work no doubt reflect the artist's observations in Arles, others come from his imagination; yet Gauguin has anchored both in the same pictorial plane. His compositions became more complex still when he began also to assign symbolic significance to the colors he used. Despite all this complexity, however, Gauguin never lost sight of the fact that his pictures needed to sell. This was the context in which he himself saw his

travels to Martinique and Tahiti and his exotic subject matter, as he explained to Émile Bernard, a fellow artist: One has to "offer the stupid buying public something new in the way of motifs" (Thomson). Even so, Gauguin's sales figures were not spectacular. Theo van Gogh represented him from 1888 on, but Theo's premature death in 1891 meant a rude awakening for Gauguin. Worse still was to follow: In that same year, the Musée du Luxembourg refused to take a work of his even as a gift. Impoverished, far away from all sponsors and patrons, Gauguin spent the rest of his days in the South Seas. All the same, his art already had its admirers among the artists themselves. The Nabis in particular, an artist group with central figures in Paul Sérusier, Paul Bonnard, and Édouard Vuillard, reacted enthusiastically to Gauguin's ideas. In a magazine article of 1890, Maurice Denis summed up Gauguin's approach, one which he himself endorsed, in the following terms: "One has to remember that a picture, before ever becoming a cavalry horse,

Vincent van Gogh, *The Mill of Blute-Fin, Montmartre*, 1886.
Oil on canvas, 18 x 14¾ in. (45.4 x 37.5 cm).
Kelvingrove Art Gallery and Museum, Glasgow, Scotland.

Vincent van Gogh, *The Bridge at Langlois*, 1888. Oil on canvas, 21¼ x 25½ in. (54 x 65 cm). Kröller-Müller Museum, Otterlo, The Netherlands.

a nude woman, or an anecdote of some kind, is essentially a plane surface covered in colored pigments that have been arranged in a particular way" (Thomson).

At the time when Paul Gauguin moved to Pont-Aven, Vincent van Gogh was only just beginning to discover Impressionism. Van Gogh had worked in the 1870s as an art dealer, a preacher, and a schoolmaster, among other things. In 1880, he finally turned to painting, initially in his Dutch homeland; after six years there he moved to join his brother Theo in Paris, where he attended the last exhibition of the independent artists and was excited by the motifs, the bright palette, and the sketch-like painting style of the Impressionists (ill. p.184). In the course of his innumerable visits to Père Tanguy's paints store, he encountered the Pointillist artists and their paintings, and networked with

Signac, Pissarro, and Guillaumin. Van Gogh exchanged works with them, put his own on show at dealers' premises, and proved his organizational ability by mounting two exhibitions for the "painters of the Petit Boulevard." This was his name for the artists of the Boulevard de Clichy, Montmartre, as distinct from the painters of the Grand Boulevard, whose works were displayed by the big-time art dealers, Durand-Ruel and Petit. Dissatisfied with his own style, and above all convinced "that a prime cause of the widespread hardship among artists is their disunity among themselves, their lack of cooperation," van Gogh turned his back on Montmartre early in 1888 (van Gogh-Bonger). He moved to Arles, in the South of France, and there he drew and painted fields, sunflowers, orchards, and vineyards—and portraits of the local people.

Over time he gradually abandoned the characteristic brush-dabs of the Impressionists and Neo-Impressionists, with their resemblance to commas and periods, replacing them with a mode of paint application that itself became a medium of expression: whirls and broad strokes in contrasting colors, sometimes applied direct from tube to canvas without use of the brush. His messages to his brother Theo requesting more paint became correspondingly frequent, all the more so because Vincent painted some two hundred pictures during the fifteen months of his stay in Arles; one of them was the famous *Bridge at Langlois* (ill. p.185). Van Gogh's dream of a harmonious colony of painters—such as he presumed to exist at Pont-Aven—ultimately came true for him in Provence. In October 1888, after months of alternately agreeing to come and deciding against, the long wished-for Gauguin arrived at the "Atelier du Midi" (Studio of the South). Van Gogh experimented with Gauguin's flat brushwork, and admired his reliance on imagination. The Frenchman did accompany him sometimes on an excursion to paint in the open air, but the tensions between these two disparate characters could not be resolved. After a quarrel at the end of the year, Gauguin moved out of the shared studio. Van Gogh had a nervous breakdown and mutilated his own left ear. In the months that followed, he suffered from sleeplessness, delusions, and the constant fear of suffering further attacks. In May 1889, he had himself admitted to the psychiatric clinic in Saint-Rémy-de-Provence. Having retired to Auvers, in the north of France, in 1890, he still further increased his already enormous rate of work, painting a picture on every day he spent there. In July of that year, after only ten years as a practicing artist, but with over 2,000 paintings and drawings to his name, van Gogh committed suicide. At the beginning of the twentieth century, the Expressionists discovered this Dutchman's art. They particularly admired the works of his final years, with their highly expressive impasto (ill. pp.186–7).

Like van Gogh, Cézanne too refused to accept that the spontaneous reproduction of an impression of nature could be an aesthetic ideal. A native of Provence, and with no successes at the Salon behind him, Cézanne had sent works to the Impressionist exhibitions of 1874 and 1877, but had been subjected to devastating reviews both times. He turned his back on Paris before either van Gogh or Gauguin, retreating to a secluded rural existence. He settled in the Midi, painting in Aix-en-Provence or L'Estaque, where he wrote to Pissarro, with whom he had often worked side by side: "This place is like a playing card, red roofs against the blue sea... . The sun here is so terrible that it seems to me as if every object stands out in silhouette, not just in black and white but in blue, in red, in brown, in violet" (*Französische Meisterwerke*). The Impressionist

Vincent van Gogh, *Woman on Tree-Lined Road*, 1889.
Oil on canvas, 12¾ x 16 in. (32.5 x 40.5 cm). Private collection.

style did not appear to him to be an appropriate way of representing such sensations on canvas, as it inhibited his talent for clearly structured, well-balanced composition.

Cézanne wanted to observe nature but at the same time study the clarity and balance of the Old Masters. Later he summed up his approach: "I wanted to make something out of Impressionism that would be as solid and enduring as the art one finds in museums" (Düchting). To this aim Cézanne dedicated himself with true passion. In the unpopulated landscapes that he painted in the open air during the 1880s, horizontals and verticals predominate. Elongated, regularly distributed brushstrokes point in all directions and create the feeling of spatial depth (ill. pp.188–9). Over a period of years, and creating about sixty paintings, drawings, and watercolors in the process, Cézanne worked on portraying one of his home region's mountains, Mont Sainte-Victoire. Increasingly he dispensed with perspective, with the graphically correct representation of the three dimensions. He created forms from the varying directions of the brushstrokes, and from the different warm and cold color tones; objects were formed from areas of color. In his still lifes and portraits too, Cézanne was trying out his artistic ideas, transferring reality to the two dimensions of the canvas (ill. p.189).

"Nature is always the same, but of its visible appearance nothing remains constant. Our art must give it the sublime attribute of permanence, along with the elements and appearance of all its changes. Art must give it eternity in our imagination. What is behind Nature? Nothing, perhaps. Perhaps everything."

Paul Cézanne, ca. 1900

Vollard was still in his early days as an art dealer when, in 1895, he presented Cézanne's œuvre in a major exhibition. The artists in particular were highly enthusiastic. Pissarro's response was one of warm admiration. Claude Monet bought two works without haggling over the price—as Vollard did not fail to point out. In the years before this exhibition, hardly any of Cézanne's art had reached the public eye, with the exception of a few pictures put on show and sold at low prices by Tanguy, the paints dealer. Cézanne was living in Provence, having dropped out of the art world completely. From now on, Vollard's gallery gradually came to establish itself as the rendezvous for Cézanne disciples, though they would also go south to visit the artist himself. Émile Bernard, a friend of Gauguin, was the first to make the journey, visiting Cézanne in Aix-en-Provence in 1904; and here Cézanne explained his artistic principles to a painter thirty years younger than himself: "To paint after nature is not to copy the objective world but to give form to one's own sensations" (Smith). Cézanne's approach to painting

As had happened already with the Impressionists and the Neo-Impressionists, artists and critics of the next trends were not short of proposals for new names. It proved possible to incorporate, into Post-Impressionism in general, labels designating the various styles that had been proliferating since as far back as the 1890s, as the painter Maurice Denis noted: he and his comrades were described as "Cloisonnists, Synthetists, Neo-Traditionalists, Ideaists, Symbolists, and Deformists." Their works were included in Fry's exhibition. It cannot be said that much stylistic common ground was discernible among the works shown, apart, perhaps, from the fact that they all dispensed with three-dimensional illusionism and any narrative content. The pieces all dated from the period 1886–1905—in other words from the period since the final Impressionist exhibition, a period during which Renoir, Monet, and Degas had all continued to practice as artists. Pablo Picasso, one more artist who had featured in Fry's exhibition, as a Post-Impressionist, returned to the study of Édouard

Paul Cézanne, *Mont Sainte-Victoire*, 1904–06. Oil on canvas, 26 x 32 in. (66 x 81.5 cm). Foundation E.G. Bührle Collection, Zürich, Switzerland.

◁ **Paul Cézanne**, *View of Mont Marseilleveyre and Maire Island*, ca. 1882–85. Oil on canvas, 20 x 24½ in. (51 x 62 cm). Private collection.

was to be followed by a host of artists. His practice of analyzing depicted objects into plane surfaces ultimately led to Cubism, and earned him the honorific of "The Father of Modern Art."

In 1910, the English art critic and exhibition promoter Roger Fry mounted a London exhibition for the painters Gauguin, van Gogh, Cézanne, Manet, and other French artists. Fry spent some time trying to think of a title for the exhibition, and finally settled on "Manet and the Post-Impressionists." He had come up with a collective name at just the right moment.

Manet and the Impressionists at a time when he was almost eighty years old. Between 1959 and 1962 he devoted himself to Manet's *"succès de scandale"* of 1863, *The Picnic*, and in the course of this study created twenty-seven painting variations and a large number of drawings and lithographs. Claude Monet's series paintings were enthusiastically praised by Wassily Kandinsky, one of the most influential artists of mainstream Modernism—and also, decades later, by the pop artist Roy Lichtenstein.

IMPRESSIONISTS IN A(U)CTION

Artists represented at the first Impressionist exhibition in 1874 could hardly complain of not receiving sufficient attention; it was cash receipts that left everything to be desired, and none of these artists are likely ever to have dreamed of the enormous sums that many collectors of our own day are prepared to pay for Impressionist art.

Vincent van Gogh, *Portrait of Dr. Gachet* (second version), 1890. Oil on canvas, 26¾ x 22½ in. (68 x 57 cm). Musée d'Orsay, Paris.

In January 1874, the textile manufacturer Ernest Hoschedé had auctioned off his collection of Impressionist pictures, obtaining thoroughly respectable prices. The critic Duret rated this auction as a major sales success for the Impressionists. In comparison, the proceeds of the first exhibition by the Société Anonyme were modest. Renoir finally succeeded in persuading his colleagues to take the way forward shown by Hoschedé's auction. Morisot, Monet, Sisley, and Renoir himself sent some seventy-three works in all to the State auction rooms in 1875. But this occasion proved a fiasco. Renoir in particular had to watch some of his pictures being knocked down for less than 100 francs, and the average price offered per picture was the modest sum of 163 francs. The results of the auction that he had brought about fell far short of the expectations of the artists involved.

The publisher Georges Charpentier took this chance to acquire Renoir's *The Angler* for 180 francs. In 1979, to the successful bidder at Sotheby's in London, that same picture was worth £610,000. Or in 1875 again, *The Theater Box* was shown at the first Impressionist exhibition and found a buyer at 220 francs. Just over three decades later, the price for this little oil painting reached 31,200 francs. And in 1989 it was auctioned once more, this time at Christie's in New York, and was duly sold. A collector paid 12.1 million dollars to return contentedly home with this canvas and its two opera-goers.

Price increases as spectacular as these must surely have exceeded all earlier expectations. They speak volumes for the esteem in which Impressionist pictures are held, especially if one compares these prices with those that the painters themselves secured during their lifetimes. In the 1870s, Monet would ask for between 1,000 and 1,500 francs for a picture, Pissarro about 500. Recalling his early days as an art dealer in the 1890s, Vollard remarked, "When I had my little shop in Rue Laffitte, Renoir prices had hardly appreciated at all, and I only ventured with some hesitancy to charge four hundred francs" (Vollard). For comparison, Renoir's *The Walk* (1870) has been rated since 1989 as a real treasure fit to grace any museum; the canvas with the strolling couple was acquired then by the Getty Museum at Malibu, California, imported from London for 17.7 million dollars. That was a mere foretaste of things to come, for a year later the Japanese industrialist Ryoei Saito bid the amazing sum of 78.1 million dollars for a smaller version of Renoir's *The Dancers at the Moulin de la Galette*. Two days earlier, moreover, the same collector had become the owner of the first version of van Gogh's *Portrait of Dr. Gachet*, for 82.5 million dollars.

The record-breaking price increases affecting the works of Renoir, van Gogh, and also Monet in the second half of the 1980s seemed to represent the high point of the international art boom of those years. Not that trading has slackened off much, even today, in the market for their pictures. Collectors, speculators, and museums continue to engage in bidding wars. Since 2002, the London market for Impressionists and for Modernist art has grown by leaps and bounds. In New York also, the location for almost half of the world's auctions, prices have risen by nearly a third over the last fifteen years. In 1999, Cézanne became the latest artist to join the line of success stories when his *Still Life with Curtain, Pitcher, and Fruit Bowl*, painted in 1893, went to

Claude Monet, *Waterloo Bridge, Fog*, 1903. Oil on canvas, 25½ x 39½ in.
(65 x 100 cm). Hermitage, St. Petersburg, Russia.

a new owner for 60.5 million dollars, paid at Sotheby's, New
York. And both Degas and Monet were among the ten highest-
turnover artists listed in the 2005 Artprice ranking.

As recently as June 2007, a Monet work narrowly missed
setting a new record, but still became the artist's second most
expensive work at 27.4 million euros, paid at Sotheby's by an
Asian collector for a waterlilies painting of 1904. This work,
one of the earliest in which Monet concentrated exclusively on
the pool surface, had been out of sight for decades past. It had
last been put on public view by its owner in 1936. This period
of absence may have stimulated competition for the canvas, as
did the fact that it is one of the last works of Monet's waterlilies
series remaining in private ownership (ill. p.180). Monet's
Nymphéas paintings have long enjoyed great popularity, and
the highest price ever paid at auction for a Monet was achieved
by another of his waterlilies paintings: *Lilypond with Waterside
Path* (1900) changed hands at Sotheby's for around 29.4 million
euros. Monet's views of Waterloo Bridge are also proving to
be likely prospects for ever-new record prices. One version
opened the London spring auctions of 2007 by going for
26 million euros.

Claude Monet in his Giverny studio, ca. 1911.

VI. IMPRESSIONISM WORLDWIDE

IMPRESSIONISM WORLDWIDE:
LONDON, NEW YORK, BERLIN...

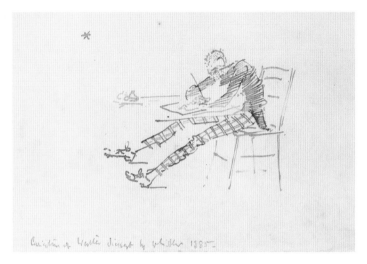

James Abbott McNeill Whistler, *Walter Richard Sickert Working on a Drawing*, 1885. Ink on paper, 4 x 6 in. (10.2 x 15.2 cm). Private collection.

"They pay no attention to draftsmanship or form, confining themselves to conveying an impression of what they call Nature. It's worse than a cabinet of horrors" (Walther II). This was the state of consternation in which Julian Alden Weir, an American student of art, wrote to his parents telling them about his visit to the first Impressionist exhibition in Paris. But after the shock of the first encounter Weir's antipathy steadily lessened, and from the 1890s he himself could be numbered among American Impressionists. Weir's change of outlook is by no means atypical of overseas reception of Impressionism.

Even though in France the demise of Impressionism was already being proclaimed, the last years of the nineteenth century saw artists in North America, Scandinavia, Britain, and Southern and Eastern Europe fired with enthusiasm for French Impressionist painting. Paris still remained the hub of the art world; in 1900 the city was still a mecca for artists, collectors, and art dealers. While in Paris new ways of seeing and painting were variously becoming established or sinking without trace, Impressionism was rippling in widening circles across the world. The traditions of French *plein-air* painting had been taken up in the second half of the nineteenth century by artists all over Europe. In most cases, art students who had been in Paris took these ideas back home—to Spain, Denmark, and North America. In Germany, it was the two principal art

centers, Berlin and Munich, that led the new enthusiasm for Impressionism. Both here and in Britain, the character of the new developments reflected efforts to break free from the French Impressionists. The judgments passed by Kaiser Wilhelm II, who regarded Impressionism as "ugly," "un-German," and "Frenchified," bear eloquent witness to national prejudice.

In this chapter, the concept of Impressionism will be anything but clear-cut; however, its "special forms" worldwide have in common their interest in light effects, enthusiasm for painting in the open air, and a free-flowing, sketch-style technique.

BRITAIN AND AMERICA

In Britain, initially, the Impressionists were less talked about than were the landscapes of the Barbizon painters, whose careers were followed with interest and whose works, on offer at Durand-Ruel's London gallery and elsewhere, were received with enthusiasm. Rustic subjects like those depicted by Millet, a member of the Barbizon school, were also a principal interest of the successful Salon painter Jules Bastien-Lepage (1848–84), whose large-format work *October* (ill. p.197) is memorable for the charm with which it depicts the two peasant women. In 1880, the Grosvenor Gallery in London exhibited Bastien-Lepage's large-format canvas showing two peasants in a field, exhausted after their day's work. *Haymaking* generated a furor; British painters were taken by storm, and hailed the painter—who had trained under Cabanel and at the École des Beaux-Arts—as an Impressionist. The younger generation of artists in Britain had found itself a master of contemporary subjects and *plein-air* painting: The influence of Bastien-Lepage would be difficult to overstate.

▷ **Mary Cassatt,** *In the Loge*, 1879.
Oil on canvas, 31½ x 25½ in. (80 x 64.8 cm).
Museum of Fine Arts, Boston, MA, U.S.,
The Hayden Collection—Charles Henry Hayden Fund.

PAGES 192–3
Joaquín Sorolla y Bastida, *Sail-Sewing* (Detail), 1896.
Oil on canvas, 86½ x 119 in. (220 x 302 cm).
Museo d'Arte Moderna Ca' Pesaro, Venice, Italy.

Philip Wilson Steer, *Poole Harbour*, 1890. Oil on canvas,
18 x 24½ in. (45.7 x 62.2 cm). City Art Gallery, Leeds, England.

▷ **Jules Bastien-Lepage**, *October*, 1878. Oil on canvas, 71¼ x 77¼ in.
(180.7 x 196 cm). National Gallery of Victoria, Melbourne, Australia.

From this point on, British artists swarmed across to France
to spend the summer in Paris or at Fontainebleau. Philip Wilson
Steer (1860–1942) matriculated at the Académie Julian in Paris
in 1882, full of enthusiasm for Bastien-Lepage's oils and in
particular inspired by his *plein-air* sketches. In the 1880s, after
returning from France, Steer often went to the Suffolk coast
to paint—in bright, unmixed pigments and with free-flowing
brushwork, though he did on occasion switch to a style showing
elements of Pointillism (ill. pp.196, 198).

Walter Richard Sickert (1860–1942) arrived in Paris in
1883, bringing with him two pictures by his mentor, Whistler,
for the Salon, and furnished with Whistler's letter of
recommendation (ill. p.194) addressed to Degas and Manet.
Under the impact of their works, Sickert concentrated on
depiction of the world of theater and variety, and also addressed
himself to pastels technique. His numerous beach scenes reveal
his penchant for unusual compositions and his preference for
the French seaside resort of Dieppe, where in 1885 he met

Degas and Monet. Sickert's oil painting *Bathers, Dieppe*
(ill. p.199), dating from about 1902, has no horizon; its figures
are grouped arbitrarily, as it seems, off-center in the picture.
The influence of Degas is clear in such paintings, as is that of
Sickert's first teacher, James Abbott McNeill Whistler (1834–
1903). An American by birth, Whistler had arrived in Paris in
1855—as had Pissarro—and had studied there at the Atelier
Gleyre, a few years ahead of the Impressionists. In 1873, he
moved to England and switched to landscape painting. Whistler
had made friends with many of the Impressionist painters,
and had been invited to take part in their first exhibition.
Whistler's *Nocturnes*, including the view of the Thames by night
(ill. pp.200–01), were painted during the 1870s. He composed
these nocturnal landscapes from large flat areas of color that he
left without definite outlines.

Open-air painting did not interest Whistler, and his
painting technique was less original than his compositions:
This confirmed studio artist filled his canvases with designs

that clung to the picture's surface level and were simplified to the point of abstraction.

"Those Englishmen who are taunted with following the methods of the French Impressionists, sneered at for imitating a foreign style, are in reality but practising their own, for the French artists simply developed a style which was British in its conception," wrote Wynford Dewhurst, author of the first English-language history of Impressionism (Impressionist Painting). It was emphasized again and again that the motifs introduced by the British Impressionists were homegrown, and that the influence of new ideas coming from France was limited to technical aspects of painting. During the years it took for French Impressionism to become established in the island kingdom, with artists and collectors alike finding their way onto the modern art scene, the indigenous landscape painters were being remembered and brought forward. Out-of-doors painting had been popular in England for decades past; such artists as John Constable (1776–1837) and William Turner (1775–1851) had gradually driven the "ideal" landscape from favor and turned instead to simple rustic motifs, underpinning their work with intensive studies of the natural world. Turner's dissolution of forms and his free-flowing brushwork impressed, notably, Monet and Sisley during their stay in London, although both denied that he had in any way influenced their own œuvre.

Philip Wilson Steer, *Knucklebones, Walberswick*, 1888–89.
Oil on canvas, 24 x 30 in. (61 x 76.2 cm).
Ipswich Borough Council Museums and Galleries, England.

▷ **Walter Richard Sickert**, *Bathers, Dieppe*, ca. 1902.
Oil on canvas, 51½ x 41 in. (131 x 104.4 cm).
Walker Art Gallery, Liverpool, England.

British artists reacted in a number of different ways to the various new impulses coming both from France and from Britain itself. They set up a common forum, the "New English Art Club," with a membership of just over fifty, among whom were Sickert and Steer. From 1886 to 1905 the Club mounted its own annual exhibition, aiming to signal its independence vis-à-vis the Royal Academy's exhibitions. Critical opinion in Britain was divided, just as the French art reviewers had been unable to agree over the early Impressionist exhibitions in Paris. It was the painting technique in particular that attracted adverse comment in Britain: *Art Journal* in 1887 referred to the "dabs-and-dots school." The reviewer concerned intended this description to include the paintings of Sargent. John Singer Sargent (1856–1925) was the son of American parents, but was reared in Europe. He embarked on the study of art in Paris in

1874, and before long met Monet. Monet's influence, occasionally even extending to the choice of subjects, is most clearly visible in works painted by Sargent during the later 1880s. Sargent never completely abandoned his taste for chiaroscuro painting, a point on which Monet and he are far apart. Nevertheless, the shared features in their works are unmistakable, at least from 1889 on.

In that same year, and coinciding with the New English Art Club exhibition, the Goupil Gallery in London put on a Monet exhibition, and *The Magazine of Art* noted indubitable links: Sargent's pictures had been painted under the direct influence of Monet, it was argued, without being on that account by any means inferior! It was not least because of his close contacts among the French Impressionists that Sargent came to be regarded as the leading British exponent of Impressionism.

In 1887, this British painter was working at Giverny, near Paris, where for some years Claude Monet had had his home. And Sargent portrayed his fellow artist much as Renoir had portrayed him at Argenteuil fifteen years earlier (ill. p.117)—at work, painting in the open air (ill. p.204). Monet is shown seated in at the forest's edge, palette in his left hand, a landscape painting on the easel in front of him, while in the background a white-clad woman reposes. Sargent gives the figures hardly any firm outlines, and dispenses almost wholly with conventional execution. His sweeping brushwork suggests rather than depicts the foliage of the trees.

At the time of Sargent's Monet portrait, American painters and American students of art were no longer an unusual sight at Giverny. When Monet first settled there, in 1883, the village population was about three hundred. Even he can hardly have envisaged the possibility that in the fullness of time more than that number of artists would follow him to Giverny. The place of abode that he had chosen for himself evolved into what was effectively a place of pilgrimage—though not solely on account of Monet's presence, as other styles flourished there in addition to Impressionism. By 1890, there were fifty practicing artists in Giverny. Between 1885 and 1915, the village as a whole was an artists' colony attracting *plein-air* painters from every country under the sun to come and do battle there with wind and weather. English artists, Austrians, Scots, Finns, Irish, Norwegians, Poles, Swedes, Canadians, and Australians were there; but the greatest numbers of artists had traveled over from the United States. In 1891, the Giverny phenomenon made it into the *New York Times*. World War I brought a major break in the Giverny story, as most of its artists left France when hostilities began. The Musée d'Art Américain, which documents the work of American artists at Giverny, opened there in 1992.

Theodore Robinson (1852–96), a painter from New York, settled down at Giverny in 1887 and discovered landscape painting for himself during the following five years. Under the influence of Monet's paintings—Robinson was one of the few artists living locally with whom Monet came to be on fairly close terms—the American gradually began to use a brighter palette and to adopt the freer, lighter style of brushwork that is to be seen, for example, in the little oil painting *The Bridge at Giverny* (ill. p.205). Like Monet, Robinson would work from photographs; like Monet, he favored series paintings.

James Abbott McNeill Whistler, *Nocturne in Blue and Silver: The Thames*, ca. 1872–78. Oil on canvas, 17½ x 24 in. (44.5 x 61 cm). Yale Center for British Art, New Haven, CT, U.S., Paul Mellon Fund.

"Why on earth shouldn't I call my works symphonies, arrangements, harmonies, nocturnes, and so on? I know there are many good people who lack a lively sense of humor and regard my nomenclature as frivolous and myself as eccentric... . But why can't they acknowledge that I mean something by it, and that I know what I mean?"
James Abbott McNeill Whistler, 1878

J.M.W. Turner, *Pont Neuf, Paris*, 1830.
Oil on canvas, 30¼ x 36¼ in. (77 x 92 cm).
Musée du Louvre, Paris.

▷ **John Singer Sargent**, *The Breakfast Table*, 1884.
Oil on canvas, 21¼ x 17¾ in. (54 x 45.1 cm). Harvard University
Art Museums, Fogg Art Museum, Cambridge, MA, U.S.

Even before returning to America in 1892, Robinson had regularly shipped work over for exhibition there and garnered a large number of awards, becoming one of the trailblazers of Impressionism in the United States; he was the first American artist to be designated in his homeland as an Impressionist. Monet might perhaps have been happy to see more painters follow Robinson's example and move away from Giverny—at least, a remark to that effect was attributed to him: "When I first came to Giverny, I was on my own and the little village was totally unspoilt. Now that so many artists and students are flocking here, I often think of moving somewhere else" (*Landschaft im Licht*).

However, a significant factor precluding any return to peaceful times was Monet's own popularity, which had grown

enormously—notably in America. At the time Monet originally moved to Giverny, his resourceful agent Paul Durand-Ruel was introducing works by Impressionist painters to an overseas public for the first time. At the International Exhibition of Art and Industry in Boston, he exhibited pictures by the French Impressionists, though with the exception of Renoir's work they failed to arouse any great enthusiasm among the critics. If the name Durand-Ruel, more than any other, is associated with the growing acceptance of Impressionism in America, the reason lies in his second trip to the United States.

This was in 1886—the year of the last Impressionist exhibition held in Paris. At the invitation of the American Art Association, Durand-Ruel shipped just under three hundred Impressionist works to New York. The consignment included

forty-eight Monets, forty-two Pissarros, thirty-eight Renoirs, twenty-two Boudins, seventeen Manets, fourteen Sisleys, seven Morisots, ten Caillebottes, three Seurats, and twenty-three works by Degas. The comprehensive Special Exhibition of Works in Oils and Pastels by the Paris Impressionists opened in March, but soon had to be transferred to a more spacious venue, having been besieged by the public and the Press who had thronged to see it. Financially, too, the show was a great success for Durand-Ruel; the pictures he sold realized $18,000. Once again it was Renoir who came off best in the reviews. However, it was Monet, not least because his works had such a massive presence in the exhibition, who came to be perceived as the leading figure of the Impressionist movement. The ground was prepared, and collectors, such as Sterling Clark, Desmond Fitzgerald, and Mr. and Mrs. Havemeyer, invested in Impressionist art while American artists set sail for France, their destination Giverny—to which

Monet's footsteps led—or to one of the Parisian academies of art.

Mary Cassatt chose the latter: like her fellow countryman, Sargent, she was to spend most of her life in Europe. On completion of her art studies in Philadelphia, she set off to travel through a number of European countries, ending up in Paris in 1873. She received instruction from Gérôme and Couture, meanwhile forming contacts among the French Impressionists. Like Degas, she would often work in the Louvre. And it was Degas who invited the young American that same year to show work at the fourth Impressionist exhibition. Cassatt saw this as a stride toward full artistic independence. For her biographer, Achille Ségard, she described her reaction to Degas' invitation: "I joyfully accepted. Now I could work completely independently, with no need to worry about what a jury might think. By now I knew who were my true masters. I admired Manet, Courbet, and Degas. I left conventional art behind me. I began to

◁ **John Singer Sargent**, *Claude Monet Painting by the Edge of a Wood*, ca. 1885.
Oil on canvas, 21¼ x 25½ in. (54 x 64.8 cm). Tate Britain, London.

Theodore Robinson, *The Bridge at Giverny*, 1891.
Oil on canvas, 10¼ x 13¾ in. (26.3 x 34.9 cm).
The Museum of Fine Arts, Houston, TX, U.S.

live" (*Landschaft im Licht*). Cassatt showed at the subsequent Impressionist exhibitions also, except for the seventh.

With Degas in particular, ten years her senior, she had a close understanding, and she also shared his enthusiasm for Japanese graphic art. Cassatt specialized in paintings with figures, preferring interiors, and family members often modeled for her (ill. pp.206–7). It may be that—perhaps influenced by Degas' working practice—she actually preferred to paint in her studio rather than out of doors, or it may be that her range of subjects tended to reflect her social role; the issue need not be pursued here. It was in Europe that her oil paintings and pastels first found an appreciative public, recognition in her American homeland not following until the 1890s, when Cassatt turned her attention increasingly to the depiction of mothers and children. In America, mainly as a result of her enthusiasm in advisory and consultative roles, Mary Cassatt left an enduring legacy: She supported the American collector Louisine Havemeyer, who together with her husband built up

a major collection that was particularly strong in figured works. Celebrated artists represented in it included, notably, Courbet, Manet, and Degas. The Havemeyer Collection, comprising almost two thousand artworks (from several centuries) eventually found a distinguished home at the Metropolitan Museum of Art in New York. In quantitative terms, its holdings of late nineteeth-century French art are today second only to those of the Musée d'Orsay in Paris.

As was to be expected in light of the impact made by Monet in the United States, the major development in American art from the 1890s onward was in Impressionistic landscape painting. Artists painted beach scenes and cityscapes to reflect their interest in light effects and atmospheric fluidity. *Plein-air* painting too had its place in the schedules of the numerous summer schools of art. These courses provided tuition in the palette choices and painting techniques of the Impressionists and Pointillists, by no means without encountering criticism. The most popular, though not the earliest, of these summer

Mary Cassatt, *Little Girl in Blue Armchair*, 1878.
Oil on canvas, 35 x 51¼ in. (89 x 130 cm).
National Gallery of Art, Mellon Collection, Washington, DC.

"Freedom is the supreme earthly good, and liberation from the tyranny of a jury is a goal worth fighting for, since no profession is more enslaved than ours."
Mary Cassatt, on first participating in an Impressionist exhibition, 1879

academies was established in 1891 by William Merritt Chase (1849–1916). His Shinnecock Summer School on Long Island, New York, became the nucleus for a colony of artists dedicated to landscape painting, and to working out of doors. Chase himself had come to Impressionism mainly by way of Manet's œuvre, and did not begin painting in the open air until the mid-1880s. In his works, especially the landscapes of the next decade, he showed the same ways of handling color and light as his French colleagues. Chase, like Degas, did not regard himself as an Impressionist: he preferred to be designated a "Realist."

Boston too was a hot spot for American Impressionism at the end of the nineteenth century. Childe Hassam (1859–1935) was born in Boston, Massachusetts, and painted in New York too.

◁ **Mary Cassatt**, *Mother and Child with Green Background*, 1887.
Pastel on paper, 21¾ x 18 in. (55 x 46 cm). Musée d'Orsay, Paris.

A qualified engraver and illustrator, he spent time in Paris in 1886 and tackled the Impressionist painting technique. Like the French Impressionists, he was fascinated by contemporary subjects. His city scenes from Boston and New York—where he made his home in 1884—show the bustling streets in varied lights and weather conditions. For Hassam, the American cities possessed as much charm as Paris: the Paris boulevards were "no whit more interesting than the streets of New York. There are days here when the sky and the atmosphere are just the same as in Paris, and the city squares and parks every bit as beautiful in their colors and grouping" (Walther II).

In 1898, Hassam joined the artist-group known as "The Ten American Painters"; later, Chase joined too. This group included both figure painters and landscape artists, and had come together in order to mount independent exhibitions: They felt the big art shows put on by the Society of American Artists were difficult to relate to, lacking in profile and focus.

Peder Severin Krøyer, *Children Bathing at Skagen Strand*, 1892.
Oil on canvas, 13 x 16 in. (33 x 40.5 cm).
Den Hirschsprungske Samling, Copenhagen.

▷ Peder Severin Krøyer, *Artists' Breakfast at Skagen*, 1883.
Oil on canvas, 32¼ x 24 in. (82 x 61 cm).
Skagens Museum, Denmark.

The parallels with the French Salon and the first Impressionist exhibition, nearly a quarter-century earlier, are unmistakable.

SCANDINAVIA

From Northern Europe too, artists were attracted to Paris. In summer the painters would take off for such places as Brittany or, perhaps, the Forest of Fontainebleau, where a group of mainly Swedish artists founded an independent artists' colony at Grèz-sur-Loing early in the 1880s. Some of these artists, returning to their home country, would bring with them their new joy in *plein-air* painting and the bright palette of the Impressionists— and also the notion of living and working among a group of artists. At Skagen, a tiny fishing hamlet on the northernmost

tip of Denmark, artists came together to paint in each other's company, far from the Academy of Art in Copenhagen. Peder Severin Krøyer (1851–1909) had traveled widely even as a young man, and had studied in Paris in his mid-twenties. From 1882 he engaged in *plein-air* painting at Skagen; a year after first arrival there, he recorded his fellow artists for posterity, assembled sociably at their *Artists' Breakfast* (ill. p.209). Among those seen at the table is the painter Christian Krohg, who had attended the seventh Impressionist exhibition the year before and been impressed by Caillebotte's pictures in particular. A number of Krøyer's pictures, some of monumental format, record Skagen's beach life too, *sur le motif*. The little 1892 canvas (ill. p.208) is a study for one of these paintings. Three children are playing in the water, reflections glint from its surface, and the white foam of the breaking waves gleams in the sunlight. Krøyer

Max Slevogt, *View of the Alster, Hamburg*, 1905.
Oil on canvas, 23¼ x 30 in. (59 x 76 cm). Alte Nationalgalerie, Berlin.

places his horizon high up in the picture, giving the seascape something of a two-dimensional character. In Paris, Krøyer's works were rated highly, and the gallery-owner Georges Petit included them in his "Expositions Internationales de Peinture" of the 1880s.

Carl Locher (1851–1915) likewise followed up a sojourn in Paris by finding his way to Skagen, where he continued to indulge his passion for seascapes (ill. p.211). Viggo Johansen (1851–1935) studied art for seven years at the Academy in Copenhagen, arriving in Skagen in 1875. As a student he had visited the fishing villages of the Zealand peninsula, and during his time at Skagen coastal landscapes continued to be the principal source of motifs for his *plein-air* studies. Later, Johansen added Impressionist and Pointillist style features to his repertoire. His works were already appearing in international exhibitions during the 1880s, and art critics rated him as an important Danish artist. Yet the influence of Impressionism remained

modest: "Stuff like this...I've never seen anything like it. All the pigments and the good canvas and the expensive frames being squandered on this rubbish... ." remarked Danish painter and art historian Karl Madsen on the second Impressionist exhibition in Paris (Walther II). And when Paul Gauguin, in 1884, attempted to make a living in Copenhagen, the responses ranged from indifference to bafflement. After no more than a year, Gauguin retreated to Paris—leaving his collection of Impressionist pictures behind with his wife. Five years later, these works were to appear in an entirely different light: Paris appeared to Madsen to be "now more than ever a world-class metropolis, with a stronger concentration of what is quintessentially modern than anywhere else" (Walther II). In 1889, alongside the pieces left behind by Gauguin, Madsen showed works by his compatriots, in an exhibition he called "Nordic and French Impressionists," at the Kunstforeningen (Art Association) in Copenhagen. He juxtaposed pictures by Manet, Degas, Cézanne, Pissarro, Sisley,

Carl Locher, *On the Beach*, 1886. Oil on canvas,
16½ x 25¾ in. (42 x 65.3 cm). Galerie G. Paffrath, Düsseldorf, Germany.

Cassatt, and Gauguin with works by Johansen, Krohg, and other Scandinavian artists. Madsen's exhibition was influential, but the number of artists choosing to adopt an impressionistic approach to painting remained small. There were, however, a number of spectacular exhibitions to follow Madsen's show. At the instigation of an artists' organization, the largest exhibition of van Goghs and Gauguins outside France was mounted in 1893—in Copenhagen!

GERMANY

France provided the yardstick, and Paris was the central hub of contemporary art. German painters, like all the others, accordingly felt the need to spend some time in the French capital or at nearby Barbizon. From about 1870 onward, a whole series of painters close to the Cologne artist Wilhelm Leibl took up landscape work. Gustave Courbet's paintings too made a distinct impact on the German artists. However, in Germany it was the historical painters that enjoyed official favor, with those such as Franz von Stuck and Franz von Lenbach calling the tune in Munich. Many artists, feeling the need for broader artistic perspectives, forsook the Bavarian capital for Berlin, where they hoped to find a more liberal political climate.

Max Liebermann (1847–1935), a Berliner by birth, traveled outside Germany initially, visiting Holland often during the 1870s. In The Hague, a group of artists with Jozef Israëls (1824–1911) as its central figure was following the lead of the Barbizon school and landscape painting outside (ill. p.214). Liebermann, influenced by The Hague school, took up *plein-air* painting and went to see Barbizon and Paris for himself. After some years in Munich, he returned to his home city of Berlin in 1884, though he soon put clear water between himself and the Academy

Max Liebermann, *Parrot Alley*, 1902.
Oil on canvas, 34¾ x 28½ in. (88.1 x 72.5 cm).
Kunsthalle Bremen, Germany.

"The only development possible for painting and for any individual
painter is toward Impressionism: this is proved by the history of art and
the history of Rembrandt or Velázquez. But Germany looks to painting
to deliver ideas, poetry, even philosophy. I want ideas too, but painterly
ones, capable of expression through form and color."
Max Liebermann, in a letter to Alfred Lichtwark, 1902

Max Liebermann, *Dunes Promenade at Noordwijk*, 1908.
Oil on wood, 24½ x 29¼ in. (62.5 x 74 cm). Kunsthalle Bremen, Germany.

exhibitions there. On his own initiative, he entered work in the Paris World's Fair of 1889, which the Prussian government was boycotting, and in subsequent years acted independently of official art policy and practice.

In 1898, a group of artists under Liebermann's chairmanship founded the "Berliner Vereinigung" (Berlin Union), which turned its back on State-controlled exhibition arrangements. Like its Munich counterpart, founded six years previously, the Berliner Vereinigung was not exclusively an Impressionist forum. Exhibitions put on by the Berlin Secession showed works by—among others—Toulouse-Lautrec, van Gogh, and Cézanne. Liebermann in any case found there was nothing to be gained from impressionistic painting using unmixed pigments: "This

business of analyzing colors is a lot of nonsense. I saw it again just now: nature is simple and gray" (Liebermann). In fact, for all his explicitly distanced attitude to the Impressionists, Liebermann's works are anything but "simple and gray." Sunbeams percolate through the dense tree canopy along Frankfurt Zoo's Parrot Alley; free-flowing brushwork and impasto characterize the beach scenes that Liebermann painted while in Holland; these visual themes leave no doubt of the artist's conviction that the decisive point is not the subject but the painterly treatment it receives (ill. pp.212–13). Liebermann considered his growing preference for modern subjects to be endorsed in the works of Manet and Degas that he began to collect—along with Monets, Renoirs, Pissarros, Sisleys, and

Jozef Israëls, *Peasant Family Returning from the Potato Harvest*, ca. 1878. Oil on canvas, 38½ x 78½ in. (97.5 x 199.5 cm). Museum of Art, Tel Aviv.

Lovis Corinth, *Portrait of the Poet Peter Hille*, 1902. Oil on canvas, 75½ x 47¾ in. (192 x 121 cm). Kunsthalle Bremen, Germany.

▷ Max Slevogt, *The Parrot Man*, 1901. Oil on canvas, 32 x 25¾ in. (81.5 x 65.3 cm). Niedersächsisches Landesmuseum, Hanover, Germany.

Cézannes—in the 1890s. In 1896 also, Liebermann and Hugo von Tschudi, Director of the National Gallery in Berlin, jointly purchased a work by Manet for the museum—with the result that Kaiser Wilhelm II, for whom Impressionism was "gutter art," made haste to prevent further acquisitions.

"Impressionism is not a movement, it is a Weltanschauung (world view)." Of this, Liebermann was convinced, and it was on the basis of this conviction that the Berlin Secession, more than any other agency, helped Impressionism to make its breakthrough in Germany around the turn of the century. Another observer of events in France was Paul Cassirer, who ran a Berlin art gallery. From the French viewpoint, the art dealer Ambroise Vollard described what was happening on the German side of the border: "Paul Cassirer's gallery seemed to be a continuation in Berlin of our Rue Laffitte. Liebermann, the Berlin-based painter, was putting our best Impressionist pictures up on his studio walls" (Vollard).

As Paul Cassirer saw it, Liebermann was one of the three members of the Berlin Secession—the others being Lovis Corinth and Max Slevogt—who constituted the "triple constellation of German Impressionism." All three engaged both in figured painting and in landscapes. Corinth (1858–1925), who hailed from East Prussia, Germany, was drawn initially to the Academy of Art at Munich. In the mid-1880s he studied at the Académie Julian in Paris, though he claimed later to have simply ignored the final Impressionist exhibition of 1886; and a considerable proportion of his work during the next few years was on paintings with religious, mythological, or historical subject matter. Back in Munich in the 1890s,

Joaquín Sorolla y Bastida, *Sail-Sewing*, 1896.
Oil on canvas, 86½ x 119 in. (220 x 302 cm).
Museo d'Arte Moderna Ca' Pesaro, Venice, Italy.

▷ Joaquín Sorolla y Bastida, *A Walk on the Beach*, 1909.
Oil on canvas, 80¾ x 78¾ in. (205 x 200 cm).
Museo Sorolla, Madrid.

Corinth took up *plein-air* landscape painting and little by little brightened his palette. In his later years it was mainly the country round the Walchensee Lake in Bavaria, scene of his family holidays from 1918 onward, that constituted his favorite landscape theme. Corinth finally settled in Berlin at the turn of the century, registering considerable successes at Cassirer's gallery in particular, and also running a profitable painting school for women. Apart from nude studies, his own œuvre consists largely of portraits. He portrayed himself forty-two times, and still found time for portraits of other people—such as the lifesize painting of Peter Hille, a poet, in 1902 (ill. p.214). Immediately after its completion, Corinth aired this portrait publicly at the fifth exhibition of the Berlin Secession, to which he had close links.

Max Slevogt (1868–1932), like Corinth, studied both in Munich and at the Académie Julian in Paris. With Corinth and others he founded the Munich Secession in 1892; he also contributed to its exhibitions. Slevogt's enthusiasm for French Impressionism—and Manet's works in particular—was

awakened only in 1900, with his visit to the World's Fair in Paris, after which Slevogt began to paint in the open air (ill. p.210). In 1901, he moved to Berlin, a move assiduously encouraged by Liebermann, but stopped off at Frankfurt am Main on the way, remaining there for quite some time. In Frankfurt's Zoological Gardens, by dint of "numerous visits to all the beasties they had"—as he told his wife—he found his subjects for a total of twenty-nine oil paintings. Three variants featured one of their keepers, the *Parrot Man* (ill. p.215). The Hanover version shows roughly sketched-in zoo visitors on a broad tree-lined promenade, the keeper standing out only because of the dark hues of his clothing. The only dabs of color in this predominantly ocher- and brown-toned painting are the gaudy feather hues of the parrots, contrasting luminously with their background. While the objects depicted are recognizable, the principal actor in this work is the sunlight streaming down through the trees.

To mark Slevogt's sixtieth birthday, the Prussian Academy of Arts in Berlin held an exhibition of his works. The painter used the catalog foreword for his "My Commitment to

Impressionism," writing, "The docile public, for whom Impressionism has always been problematic, is only too happy to see it as an approach to art that—so it believes—dispenses with art, to see it as a mere way of transferring retinal images to canvas, and at best only an extension to the laws of optics... Anyone incapable of seeing color in real life has no chance of seeing a picture that has been painted impressionistically" (*Slevogt und seine Zeit*).

SPAIN

Édouard Manet's enthusiasm for Spanish painting, for the works of Velázquez and Goya, reflects the wave of intoxication with things Spanish that affected mid-nineteenth-century France. But there was some reciprocity of interest. During a stay in France, again around the middle of the century, the painter Carlos de Haes (1826–98), who was born in Belgium and grew

Ramon Casas i Carbó, *Out of Doors*, 1892.
Oil on canvas, 20 x 26 in. (51 x 66 cm).
Museo Nacional d'Arte de Catalunya, Barcelona, Spain.

▷ Mariano Fortuny y Marsal, *The Artist's Children in a Japanese Drawing-Room*, 1874. Oil on canvas, 17¼ x 36½ in. (44 x 93 cm). Museo del Prado, Casón del Buen Retiro, Madrid.

up in Spain, encountered the out-of-doors painting tradition at Barbizon. Subsequently, as a lecturer at the Academy of Fine Arts in Madrid, he established the practice of *plein-air* painting there, and his numerous students were in large measure responsible for the steady growth in popularity of landscape painting in nineteenth-century Spain. In 1874, the year of the first Impressionist exhibition in Paris, Aureliano de Beruete (1845–1912), from Madrid, became one of de Haes' students and began to develop his impressionistic style of painting.

The same year saw the death of the Catalan painter Mariano Fortuny y Marsal (1838–74). He was famous for his historical pictures and small-format genre paintings, and in addition was a keen "pleinairist." Fortuny had spent a long time in Paris; during his stay there, Fortuny himself had developed a passionate interest in Japanese art. He began to collect the graphic art and books of Japanese artists; motifs from these sources found their way into his own works, including one of the last of them, the unfinished portrait

of his two children in an interior featuring Japanese décor (ill. p.219). Fortuny's enthusiasm for Japanese graphic art prints, his way of reproducing light and color, and above all the free-flowing style of his brushwork were incidentally responsible for the rapid development of contacts between French art critics and the emerging Impressionist painters.

However, the Impressionists' art did not particularly impress Joaquín Sorolla y Bastida (1863–1923), a native of Valencia, when he was staying in Paris in 1885. Like many of the British artists, he was more attracted by the works of Bastien-Lepage. Sorolla found that he could relate to this tradition, and set himself to painting large-format historical pictures on contemporary subjects. It was with such works that he achieved his first major successes in Spain—which did not prevent him, however, from abandoning his realism and its defining characteristic of light–dark contrasts. His creative work now came more under the influence of contemporary painting in Valencia, in which bold colors and rapid brushstrokes had become established.

Sorolla responded to the painting style and the luminous palette of such artists as Antonio Muñoz Degrain, Emilio Sala, and Francisco Domingo, incorporating these into depictions of subjects that he found in his immediate surroundings—Valencian fisherfolk and children on the beach. His painting *Sail-Sewing* of 1896 (ill. p.216) bears witness to the new pictorial language, in which the two dominating elements are the impression of snapshot spontaneity and the intense Mediterranean light. The reviewers initially found Sorolla's

pretty, too dependent on market appeal. A similar development affected the reception of Monet's series pictures.

The influence of French Impressionism is most vividly apparent further north from Valencia, in the border province of Catalonia. In 1889, Santiago Rusiñol (1861–1931) set out from Barcelona for Paris, more precisely Montmartre, where the friends he made included Toulouse-Lautrec. Rusiñol took part in the Paris Salon of Independent Artists in 1891; together with his Spanish colleague Casas he also mounted exhibitions

composition over-bold in that, in a sense, it makes the sailcloth into the principal actor. But Sorolla had found his own style: He subsequently remained faithful to the large-format approach, one that the French Impressionists seldom ventured to try. The attention to detail that had characterized Sorolla's early work now gave way to a more sketch-like style of painting with which, mostly observing from a high vantage-point, he endeavored to capture the Mediterranean light on his canvas. It was in Paris, of all places, that Sorolla achieved his international breakthrough: At the 1900 World's Fair there, he received the Grand Prix of Spain and Portugal; and six years later the Parisian gallery-owner Petit accorded him an exhibition.

In the meantime, Sorolla was painting brightly colored, luminous beach pictures of Jávea, El Cabañal, Valencia, Biarritz, and San Sebastian—and, in spite of their large format, was doing so *en plein air*. In these works his subject seems to be the light, to the exclusion of all else—the light whose rays he often chose to have additionally reflected by parasols or sails. Enthusiasm for Sorolla's "luminismo," his light-painting, fell away at first after his death in 1923, the feeling being that his paintings were too

on his own account. In addition, Rusiñol was active as an art critic and a dramaturge; he painted portraits and cityscapes, but above all is remembered as one of the most important of Catalan landscape painters. After returning to Spain, he devoted himself from the turn of the century onward solely to the gardens and parks of his homeland, traveling constantly in it until his death. The gardens of Montmartre, by contrast, were one of the locations chosen by Ramon Casas i Carbó (1866–1932), whose painting *Out of Doors* (ill. p.218) testifies to his enthusiasm for the Impressionist painting method—even if Casas favored the relatively dark palette of the Spanish painters. In 1897, Casas and Rusiñol, together with other artists, opened a café-bar that they called "Els Quatre Gats" in their home city of Barcelona. In a similar fashion to the Paris variety café "Le Chat Noir" that served as its model, "Els Quatre Gats" evolved into an artists' rendezvous. Casas and Rusiñol were not the only painters to exhibit there, for it became established as an exhibition center for a range of artists. A certain Pablo Picasso did the illustrations for the menu cards, and in 1899 could still find space on its walls to pin up his first artworks... .

INDEX OF WORKS ILLUSTRATED
(The abbreviation FO indicates a fold-out plate)

FURTHER READING

Adams, Steven: *The Barbizon School & the Origins of Impressionism*, London 1994

Arnold, Matthias: *Claude Monet*, Reinbek bei Hamburg 1998

Baudelaire, Charles: *"The Painter of Modern Life,"* in: *Essays on Literature and Art*. 1857–1860, Collected Works, Vol. 5, pp. 368–83

Blunden, Maria: *Impressionists and Impressionism*, Stuttgart 1976

Castagnary, Jules: *Salons (1857–1870)*, Paris 1892

Coll, Isabel: Ramon Casas. *Catálogo razonado*, Murcia 2002

Cugini, Carla: "Er sieht einen Fleck, er malt einen Fleck." Physiologische Optik, Impressionismus und Kunstkritik, Basel 2006

Dippel, Andrea: *Impressionismus*, Cologne 2002

Distel, Anne: *Impressionism: The First Collectors*, New York 1990

Droste-Hennings, Julia; Droste, Thorsten: *Paris. Eine Stadt und ihr Mythos*, Ostfildern 2005

Düchting, Hajo: *Seurat*, Cologne 2000

Düchting, Hajo: *Paul Cézanne*, Cologne 2003

Edelstein, T.J. (ed.): *Perspectives on Morisot*, New York 1990

Födermayr, Franz: *"Klangfarbe,"* in: *Die Musik in Geschichte und Gegenwart*, Cassel 1996, pp. 138–69

García-Bermejo, José María Faerna: *Sorolla*, Madrid 2006

van Gogh-Bonger, Johanna Gezina (ed.): *Vincent van Goghs Briefe an seinen Bruder*, 3 vols, Frankfurt am Main 1988

Growe, Bernd: *Degas*, Cologne 2001

Heinrich, Christoph: *Monet*, Cologne 2007

Kabisch, Thomas: *"Impressionismus,"* in: *Die Musik in Geschichte und Gegenwart*, Cassel 1996, pp. 526–35

Krems, Eva-Bettina: *Der Fleck auf der Venus*, Munich 2003

McConkey, Kenneth: *British Impressionism*, London 1998

Mainardi, Patricia: *Art and Politics of the Second Empire: the Universal Expositions of 1855 and 1867*, New Haven, London 1987

Mainardi, Patricia: *The End of the Salon: Art and the State in the Early Third Republic*, New York and Cambridge 1993

Renoir, Edmond: *Mein Bruder Pierre-Auguste Renoir. Der Brief von 1879*, Basel 2007

Rewald, John: *History of Impressionism*, Cologne 2001

Roos, Jane Mayo: *Early Impressionism and the French State, 1866–1874*, Cambridge 1996

Smith, Paul: *Impressionism: Beneath the Surface*, Cologne 1995

Thomson, Belinda: *Impressionism: Origins, Practice, Reception*, London 2000

Thomson, Belinda: *Post-impressionism*, 1998

Vollard, Ambroise: *Erinnerungen eines Kunsthändlers*, Zurich 1980

Walther, Ingo F. (ed.): *Malerei des Impressionismus*, 2 vols, Cologne 1992

Weitzenhoffer, Frances: *The Havemeyers. Impressionism Comes to America*, New York 1986

Wolf, Norbert: *Kunst-Epochen. 19. Jahrhundert*, Stuttgart 2002

Zola, Émile: *Écrits sur l'Art*

Exhibition Catalogs

Französische Meisterwerke des 19. Jahrhunderts aus dem Metropolitan Museum of Art, New York, Neue Nationalgalerie, Berlin, 2007

Gauguin and the Origins of Symbolism by Guillermo Solana, Richard Shiff, Guy Cogeval, and Maria Dolores Jiménez-Blanco, London, 2005

Giverny impressioniste. Une Colonie d'Artistes, 1885–1915, Musée d'Art Américain – Terra Foundation for American Art, Giverny, 2007

Musée d'Orsay: 100 Impressionist Masterpieces by Madeline Laurence, London, 1999

Quotations used are referenced by brief title, author surname, and where necessary the publication date. In the case of exhibition catalogs, the principal title element serves as title reference.

PICTURE CREDITS

© akg images, Berlin: 12–13, 22 (Erich Lessing), 34 (Erich Lessing), 35, 56, 78 bottom, 85 bottom, 89, 102, 128, 129 left, 129 right, 137 (Erich Lessing), 138, 204, 206 (Erich Lessing), 213, 214 top, Fold out: 3 center, 3 right (Joseph S. Martin), 4 center, 4 right, 5 right, 6 center, 6 right (RIA Nowosti)

© Archives Charmet/Bridgeman Berlin: 82

© Artothek, Weilheim: 4, 6–7, 9, 42–3, 46, 88, 93, 109, 133, 158, 191 top, 211

© Bibliothèque Nationale, Paris: 170

© Blauel/Artothek, Weilheim: 215

© Blauel/Gnamm/Artothek, Weilheim: 62 bottom, 185, 214 bottom

© Bridgeman Berlin: cover, 2, 8, 10–11, 17, 18–19, 20, 23, 24, 30, 32, 33, 36–7, 38, 39, 40, 41, 44–5, 48–9, 51, 54, 56–7, 59, 60–61, 64, 68 bottom, 69, 70, 71, 72–3, 76, 77, 80–81, 84, 85 top, 86–7, 91, 98, 104, 105, 106–7, 108, 112, 113, 116, 117, 118, 119, 120, 124–5, 125, 130–31, 134, 136, 141, 142, 143, 152, 153, 154, 155, 156 top right, 157, 161, 162–3, 164, 165, 166 top, 166 bottom, 168–9, 172, 174, 175, 176, 177, 180, 182, 183, 186–7, 188–9, 189, 190, 202, 207, 208, 209, 210, 217, 219, Fold out: 1, 6 left

© Brooklyn Museum of Art, New York/Bridgeman Berlin: Fold out: 8

© Brooklyn Museum of Art, New York/Gift of A. Augustus Healy/Bridgeman Berlin: 178–9

© Christie's Images/Artothek, Weilheim: 28–9, 65, 135, 146, 147, 173

© Christie's Images/Bridgeman Berlin: 167 bottom

© Corbis, Düsseldorf: 191 bottom

© Ursula Edelmann/Artothek, Weilheim: 62 top

© Fine Art Society, London/Bridgeman Berlin: 194

© Fitzwilliam Museum, University of Cambridge, UK/Bridgeman Berlin: 83, 160, Fold out: 5 left

© Fogg Art Museum, Harvard University Art Museums/Bequest from the Collection of Maurice Wertheim, Class 1906, Cambridge (MA)/Bridgeman Berlin: Fold out: 5 center

© Fogg Art Museum, Harvard University Art Museums/Bequest of Grenville L. Winthrop, Cambridge (MA)/Bridgeman Berlin: 203

© Fred Jones Jr. Museum of Art, University of Oklahoma/Aaron M. and Clara Weitzenhoffer Bequest, 2000/Bridgeman Berlin: 156 top left

© Glasgow City Council (Museums)/Bridgeman Berlin: 90, 97, 184

© Gnamm/Artothek, Weilheim: 121

© Haags Gemeentemuseum, Den Haag/Bridgeman Berlin: 78 top

© Held Collection/Bridgeman Berlin: 68 top

© Imagno/Artothek, Weilheim: 25, 47, 74–5, 156 bottom

© Ipswich Borough Council Museums and Galleries, Ipswich (Suffolk)/Bridgeman Berlin: 198

© Leeds Museums and Galleries (City Art Gallery)/Bridgeman Berlin: 196

© Lefevre Fine Art Ltd., London/Bridgeman Berlin: 148 bottom

© Joseph S. Martin/Artothek, Weilheim: 79 bottom, 122

© Metropolitan Museum of Art/Art Resource/Scala, Florence: 66–7

© Musée Marmottan, Paris,/Bridgeman Berlin: 52–3, 140, 181, Fold out: 2–7, 3 left

© Museo d'Arte Moderna Ca' Pesaro, Venice/Bridgeman Berlin: 192–3, 216

© Museo Nacional d'Arte de Catalunya, Barcelona/Bridgeman Berlin: 218

© Museum of Art, Santa Barbara (CA)/Bridgeman Berlin: 110–11

© Museum of Fine Arts/Bequest of Alexander Cochrane, Boston (MA)/Bridgeman Berlin: 150–51

© Museum of Fine Arts/Gift of Audrey Jones Beck, Houston (TX)/Bridgeman Berlin: 159

© Museum of Fine Arts/The Hayden Collection–Charles Henry Hayden Fund, Boston (MA)/Bridgeman Berlin: 195

© Museum of Fine Arts/Wintermann Collection, Gift of Mr & Mrs D. R. Wintermann, Houston (TX)/Bridgeman Berlin: 205

© National Gallery of Victoria, Melbourne/Felton Bequest/Bridgeman Berlin: 197

© Nationalmuseum, Stockholm / Bridgeman Berlin: 31

© Roger-Viollet, Paris/Bridgeman Berlin: 55

© Samuel Courtauld Trust, Courtauld Institute of Art, Gallery, London/Bridgeman Berlin: 144–5

© Sotheby's/akg-images, Berlin: 35 left, 177

© Southampton City Art Gallery, Hampshire/Bridgeman Berlin: Fold out: 4 left

© State Hermitage Museum, St. Petersburg: 94–5

© Stern Art Dealers, London/Bridgeman Berlin: 167 top

© Walker Art Gallery, National Museums Liverpool/Bridgeman Berlin: 199

© G. Westermann/Artothek, Weilheim: 212

© Peter Willi/Artothek, Weilheim: 14–15, 16, 26–7, 50, 63, 79 top, 92, 96, 99, 100–01, 103, 114–15, 123, 126–7, 141, 148 top, 149, 171

© Yale Center for British Art, Paul Mellon Fund, New Haven (CT)/Bridgeman Berlin: 200–01

This is a Parragon Publishing Book

This edition published in 2009

Parragon Books Ltd
Queen Street House
4 Queen Street
Bath BA1 1HE, UK

Copyright © Parragon Books Ltd 2008

ISBN: 978-1-4075-4274-4

Printed in China

German edition created and produced by:
Michael Konze, Lioba Waleczek, Cologne
Design: Elisabeth Hardenbicker, Cologne
Reproduction: farbo prepress, Cologne

US edition produced by:
Cambridge Publishing Management Ltd
Project editor: Penny Isaac
Translation: Richard Elliott and Michael Loughridge
Typesetter: Julie Crane
Copy editor: Nina Hnatov
Proofreader: Karolin Thomas

Ill. p.2
Pierre-Auguste Renoir, *La Grenouillère* (detail), 1869. Oil on canvas, 25½ x 36¼ in. (65.1 x 92.1 cm). Kunstmuseum, Winterthur, Switzerland.

Ill. p.4
Mary Cassatt, Self-Portrait, ca. 1880. Watercolor on paper, 13 x 9½ in. (33 x 24.4 cm). National Portrait Gallery, Washington, DC.

Artist Biographies

1865 — Degas and Monet first exhibit at the Salon.

1866 — Monet's portrait *Camille* or *The Woman in a Green Dress* (ill. p.51) is a success at the Salon.

1867 — Bazille purchases Monet's picture *Women in the Garden*. On August 8, Camille gives birth to Monet's son, Jean. Sisley's son Pierre is born.

Alfred Sisley, *The Chestnut Avenue near La-Celle-Saint-Cloud*, 1867. Oil on canvas, 37½ x 48 in. (95.5 x 122 cm). City Art Gallery, Southampton, England.

1869 — Degas and Manet paint at Boulogne-sur-Mer. During the summer, Monet and Renoir exhibit at Bougival, France.

1870 — Claude Monet and Camille marry on June 28. Monet paints beach scenes at Trouville, France. As the Franco-Prussian War approaches, Monet escapes to London and there meets Pissarro. Both become acquainted with Durand-Ruel, the art dealer. Frédéric Bazille, serving on the front line, is killed in action on November 28.

1872 — Degas travels to London, then on to New Orleans, Louisiana. Manet paints at Argenteuil. His *Impression: Sunrise* (ill. p.9) results from work at Le Havre. Durand-Ruel buys his first Renoir.

1873 — Monet meets Gustave Caillebotte. Renoir takes part in the Salon des Refusés. Foundation of the "Société Anonyme"; members include Degas, Monet, Morisot, Renoir, and Pissarro.

1875 — Auction of Impressionist pictures at the Hôtel Drouot in Paris.

1876 — Monet meets the collector Victor Chocquet. Caillebotte takes part in the second Impressionist exhibition.

1877 — Manet paints *Nana* (ill. p.121) inspired by the heroin of *L'Assommoir* by Zola published the same year. Death of Gustave Courbet, December 31.

1878 — The Musée des Beaux-Arts in Paris buys a Degas work for 2,000 francs. Monet's family moves to Vétheuil, France. Renoir takes part in the Salon. Seurat begins his studies at the École des Beaux-Arts. Charles-François Daubigny dies in Paris, February 19.

Culture

1867 The Goncourt brothers publish their novel *Manette Salomon*.

1869 In Munich, the First International Exhibition of Art is held. Leo Tolstoy publishes *War and Peace*. Flaubert's *L'Education sentimentale* appears. Paris's first music hall opens: the Folies Bergères.

1871 Émile Zola starts on his twenty-volume novel cycle about the Rougon-Macquart family. Foundation stone laid for the Semper Opera at Dresden.

1872 Construction of the Bayreuth Opera House begins.

1873 Publication of Jules Verne's novel *Around the World in Eighty Days*.

1874 The first Impressionist exhibition opens. Zola publishes *Le Ventre de Paris (The Belly of Paris)*.

1875 Construction begins on Sacré-Coeur in Paris. World premiere of Georges Bizet's opera *Carmen* in Paris. Opening of the Grand Opéra in Paris.

1876 Second Impressionist exhibition. First performance of Richard Wagner's Ring cycle in Bayreuth. Publication of *The Adventures of Tom Sawyer* by Mark Twain.

1877 Third Impressionist exhibition. Tolstoy publishes his novel *Anna Karenina*. Friedrich Nietzsche publishes *Human, All too Human: A Book for Free Spirits*.

1879 Fourth Impressionist exhibition. Zola's novel *Nana* is serialized in the daily *Le Voltaire*. The Société d'Aquarellistes Français holds its first exhibition.

1880 Fifth Impressionist exhibition. The State passes responsibility for the Salon to the Société des Artistes Français. Rodin completes *Le Penseur (The Thinker)* and starts work on *La Porte de l'enfer (The Gates of Hell)*.

1881 Sixth Impressionist exhibition. Jacques Offenbach's opera *The Tales of Hoffmann* premieres at the Opéra Comique in Paris.

1882 Seventh Impressionist exhibition in Rue St.-Honoré. Premiere of Wagner's *Parsifal*, Bayreuth. Founding of the Union des Femmes Peintres et Sculpteurs.

Rodin, *Le Penseur*, 1880. Bronze, 28¼ in. (72 cm). Musée Rodin, Paris.

History

1864 Founding of the Red Cross in Geneva and of the First Communist International in London.

Assassination of Abraham Lincoln by John Wilkes Booth, April 14, 1865. Contemporary wood engraving.

1865 Assassination of President Lincoln in the United States. Mendel formulates his laws of heredity.

1867 Austria-Hungary becomes a Double Monarchy. Garibaldi marches on Rome. Second Paris World's Fair. Publication of Karl Marx's *Das Kapital*. Emperor Maximilian captured and shot in Mexico.

1868 Opening of the Bibliothèque Nationale in Paris. The Saint-Lazare railroad station in Paris is enlarged. Queen Isabella II of Spain is deposed and forced into exile in France.

1869 Opening of the Suez Canal.

1870 Outbreak of the Franco-Prussian War. Napoleon III abdicates. Construction of the Brooklyn Bridge, New York, begins.

1871 Paris surrenders to the Prussians. Proclamation of the Paris Commune in March, followed by its suppression during the "Bloody Week" at the end of May. End of the Second Empire. Wilhelm I is proclaimed German Emperor at Versailles.

1873 World's Fair held in Vienna. Napoleon III dies in London. Banking crash and worldwide financial crisis. Marshal MacMahon becomes President of France.

1875 French National Assembly retrospectively approves the Constitution of the Third Republic, in existence since 1871.

1876 World's Fair in Philadelphia. Alexander Graham Bell patents the telephone.

1878 Third Paris World's Fair. The First International Congress for Women's Rights is also held in Paris.

1880 The anniversary of the storming of the Bastille, July 14, is declared the French national day of celebration. France annexes Tahiti.

Artist Biographies	Culture	History

Artist Biographies

1830 **Camille Pissarro** born July 10 on the Caribbean island of St. Thomas.

1832 **Édouard Manet** born January 23.

1834 **Hilaire-Germaine-Edgar de Gas** (Degas) is born in Paris. **James Abbott McNeill Whistler** is born in Massachusetts, U.S.

1839 **Paul Cézanne** born January 19; **Alfred Sisley** October 30.

1840 Birth of **Claude Monet**, November 14.

1841 Birth in France of **Pierre-Auguste Renoir**; **Frédéric Bazille**; **Berthe Morisot**.

1844 **Mary Stevenson Cassatt** born in Pittsburgh, U.S.

1848 **Paul Gauguin** born June 7; **Gustave Caillebotte** August 19.

1853 Degas matriculates as a law student at the University of Paris. **Vincent van Gogh** is born at Groot-Zundert, The Netherlands.

1855 Degas attends the École des Beaux-Arts.

1859 Degas returns from Italy to Paris and continues work on *Portrait of the Bellelli Family*. Monet moves to Paris, registers as a student at the Académie Suisse, and meets Pissarro. **Georges-Pierre Seurat** is born in Paris, December 2.

Claude Monet, *Caricature of Jules Husson, "Champfleury,"* 1858. Pencil and gouache on paper, 12½ x 9½ in. (32 x 24 cm). Musée Marmottan, Paris.

1861 Manet exhibits at the Salon for the first time. Monet is called up for military service in Algeria. A year later, he returns on sick leave and his aunt buys him out six years early.

1862 Renoir attends the École des Beaux-Arts. Monet paints on the Normandy coast, accompanied by Boudin and Jongkind. In November, Monet works in the Paris studio of Charles Gleyre, where he meets Sisley, Renoir, and Bazille.

1863 Monet, Sisley, Renoir, and Bazille paint in the countryside at Barbizon, in the Forest of Fontainebleau. Manet enters his work *Le déjeuner sur l'herbe* (ill. p.41) for the Salon des Refusés. **Joaquín Sorolla y Bastida** is born in Valencia. Death of Eugène Delacroix in Paris, August 13. Birth of **Paul Signac** in Paris, November 11.

1864 Renoir exhibits at the Salon for the first time. Bazille and Monet work at Honfleur, Normandy.

Culture

1843 The world's first nightclub, "Le Bal des Anglais," opens in Paris.

1847 Max Liebermann born July 20.

1852 Alexandre Dumas publishes his novel *La Dame aux camélias (The Lady with the Camelias)*.

1853 Giuseppe Verdi composes his opera *La Traviata*.

1854 The Brothers Grimm publish the first volume of their *German Dictionary*.

1855 Courbet puts on his own exhibition in Paris under the title of "Le Réalisme." Karl Baedeker's travel guide *Paris and Environs* is published.

Gustave Courbet, *The Meeting* or *Bonjour Monsieur Courbet*, 1854. Oil on canvas, 52 x 59¼ in. (132 x 150.5 cm). Musée Fabre, Montpellier, France.

1856 **Sigmund Freud** born at Příbor (at that time Freiberg, Moravia).

1857 Completion of the Bois de Boulogne and the Longchamp racecourse. Charles Baudelaire's poetry volume *Les Fleurs du mal* appears, as does Gustave Flaubert's novel *Madame Bovary*.

1859 Launch of the art journal *Gazette des Beaux-Arts*. Charles Darwin publishes *On the Origin of Species*.

1860 Jacob Burckhardt publishes *The Civilization of the Renaissance*.

1861 In England, William Morris founds the Arts and Crafts movement.

1862 Construction work begins on the Paris Opera House under the direction of Charles Garnier. Victor Hugo's novel *Les Misérables* published. Birth of **Claude Debussy**, August 22.

1864 Founding of the Union Centrale des Arts Décoratifs for the promotion of arts and crafts in France.

1866 Publication of Fyodor Dostoevsky's novel *Crime and Punishment*. Alphonse Daudet publishes his *Lettres de mon moulin*.

History

1830 July Revolution in France. Charles X abdicates. Louis Philippe I is proclaimed king by the bourgeoisie.

1833 With the first Factory Act, England attempts to alleviate the dreadful working conditions in the textile industry.

1843 France extends its colonial possessions in Africa and Oceania.

1845 In England, Thomas Cook founds the world's first travel agency.

1848 February Revolution in Paris, abdication of the "bourgeois king." A Republic is proclaimed. March Revolution in Germany; revolutions in Vienna, Hungary, and Italy. Marx and Engels publish the *Communist Manifesto*.

1851 Coup d'état by the French President, Louis Napoleon.

1852 End of the Second Republic. Louis Napoleon is crowned Emperor of France. The Prefect of the Département of the Seine, Baron Haussmann, initiates the *"grands travaux,"* the reconstruction of Paris. The first department store in Paris, Le Bon Marché, is founded.

1853 The Crimean War begins as a dispute between Russia and the Ottoman Empire. France, Great Britain, and Piedmont-Sardinia line up with the latter.

1855 The first World's Fair is staged in Paris.

1856 Crimean War ends with a peace treaty signed in Paris. The United States concludes the first treaty ever signed between any Western nation and Japan. Opening of the railroad linking Paris to Fécamp.

Horace Vernet, *The Storming of Sebastopol on September 8, 1855*, 1858. Oil on canvas, 24 x 18 in. (61 x 46 cm). Musée Rolin, Autun, France.

1860 Abraham Lincoln becomes U.S. President.

1861 Outbreak of the U.S. Civil War. Wilhelm I becomes King of Prussia. The Tsar of Russia, Alexander II, abolishes serfdom.

1862 World's Fair in London. Alfred Nobel uses nitroglycerine as an explosive.

1863 The first ever underground railroad opens in London. The rail line linking Paris and Trouville is opened.

Artist Biographies	Culture	History

Artist Biographies

1891 Georges Seurat dies in Paris, March 29.

1892 Durand-Ruel mounts a Degas exhibition. Monet works on the Rouen Cathedral series, and marries Alice Hoschedé.

1894 Cézanne visits Monet at Giverny. In September, Renoir's son Jean is born. The French State purchases a painting by Berthe Morisot. Gustave Caillebotte dies, February 21.

1895 Berthe Morisot dies in Paris, March 2.

1897 Monet has a second studio built for him in Giverny and paints his first water lilies pictures. Sisley marries his partner, Marie Lesouezec.

1899 Death of Alfred Sisley, January 29. Monet begins his series of River Thames views.

1903 Gauguin dies in the Marquesas Islands, May 8. Whistler dies in London, July 17. Camille Pissarro dies in Paris, November 13. Renoir settles at Cagnes-sur-Mer.

1906 Death of Paul Cézanne, October 22.

1907 Manet's *Olympia* (ill. pp.44–5) is hung in the Louvre.

Aureliano de Beruete, *The Banks of the Manzanares*, 1912. Oil on canvas, 22½ x 32 in. (57 x 81 cm). Museo del Prado, Madrid.

1917 Edgar Degas dies, September 27. In December, Henri Matisse visits Renoir at Cagnes-sur-Mer.

1919 Pierre-Auguste Renoir dies at Cagnes, December 3.

1921 The French State offers the Orangerie in the Tuileries as the setting in which to hang Monet's *Waterlilies* gift.

1923 Duncan Phillips, a Washington art collector, buys Renoir's painting *Luncheon of the Boating Party* (ill. p.141) from Durand-Ruel.

1926 Monet dies at Giverny, December 5.

1935 Death of Max Liebermann in Berlin, February 8; Paul Signac dies in Paris, August 15.

Culture

1907 The New York Metropolitan Museum of Art purchases Renoir's *Madame Charpentier and her Children* (ill. p.142). Pablo Picasso paints *Les "Demoiselles" d'Avignon*.

1909 Robert Edwin Peary becomes the first person to reach the North Pole.

1911 Wassily Kandinsky publishes the treatise *On the Spiritual in Art*. Ernest Rutherford develops his theory of the structure of the atom. Roald Amundsen reaches the South Pole.

1912 Publication of Thomas Mann's story *Death in Venice*.

1913 Exhibition of modern art at the Armory Show in New York. Nils Bohr develops the atomic model named after him, creating the theoretical basis for nuclear physics.

1914 In Cologne, the Deutscher Werkbund (German Craftwork League) holds an exhibition devoted to "Industrial Design."

1915 Kasimir Malevich publishes his *Suprematist Manifesto*.

1917 Founding of the Netherlands artist group De Stijl.

1922 James Joyce publishes *Ulysses*.

1925 First Surrealist exhibition. In the United States, Chaplin makes *The Gold Rush*.

1929 The New York Metropolitan Museum of Art receives what remains its largest endowment ever: the H.O. Havemeyer Collection.

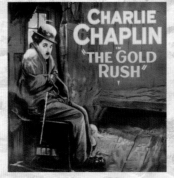

Film poster advertising Charlie Chaplin's *The Gold Rush*, U.S., 1925.

History

1904 The Nobel Prize for medicine goes to Ivan Petrovich Pavlov. Franco-British "Entente Cordiale" aims to establish peaceful coexistence between the two countries.

1905 Albert Einstein develops the theory of relativity. First Russian Revolution.

1908 Austria occupies Bosnia and Herzegovina. Tel Aviv founded.

1910 Japan annexes Korea. China abolishes slavery.

1914 Assassination in Sarajevo of the heir to the Austrian throne. Outbreak of World War I.

1915 Italy declares war on Austria. French offensive in the Champagne region.

1916 In the battle for Verdun, German and French troops confront each other through months of stalemate.

1917 February Revolution takes place in Russia. President Wilson of the US declares war on Germany.

1918 U.S. President Wilson presents his "Fourteen Points." The end of World War I is marked by an armistice between the Allies and Germany. Kaiser Wilhelm II abdicates, and Germany is proclaimed a republic.

Lenin proclaims the victory of the Revolution on November 8, 1917. Painting by Vladimir Alexandrovich Serov.

1919 Peace Conference at Versailles.

1920 The League of Nations begins work.

1922 Founding of the Soviet Union. Benito Mussolini marches on Rome.

1925 Locarno Conference. Conclusion of security pacts between Germany and its neighbors.

1929 New York stock market crashes on "Black Friday," October 25.

1933 On January 30, Adolf Hitler becomes German Chancellor. With the Enabling Act of March 24, the National Socialist dictatorship is established.

	Artist Biographies	**Culture**	**History**

1879 Mary Cassatt's debut appearance in an Impressionist exhibition, the fourth. Death of Camille Monet, September 5.

1880 Monet exhibits at the Salon and in rooms provided by *La Vie moderne* magazine.

1881 Renoir paints in Algeria during the spring, travels to Italy in the fall. Monet spends spring and summer working in Normandy. Manet is made a Chevalier de la Légion d'Honneur.

Edgar Degas, *Arabesque over the Right Leg*, ca. 1882–95. Wax, height about 8 in. (20 cm). The Fitzwilliam Museum, Cambridge, England.

1883 Monet's first one-man exhibition, held at Durand-Ruel's gallery. Manet dies on April 30. Monet moves to Giverny. As the year closes, Renoir and Monet visit Cézanne in L'Estaque, Provence.

1884 Manet memorial exhibition held in the École des Beaux-Arts.

1885 Renoir's son Pierre born March 21. Renoir settles near Giverny. The Paris gallery owner Georges Petit exhibits works by Monet and others.

1886 Monet takes part in an exhibition in Brussels organized by the artist group Les XX. Seurat puts his *A Sunday Afternoon on the Island of La Grande Jatte* (ill. pp.162–3) on display.

1888 Monet paints on the Côte d'Azur. Works by him are shown in June by the Boussod & Valadon gallery in Paris. Monet declines to be appointed to the Légion d'Honneur.

1889 Monet has works on display at the Paris World's Fair. Major retrospective of Monet and Rodin held at Petit's gallery. Monet organizes a subscription campaign aimed at buying Manet's *Olympia* (ill. pp.44–5) for the nation.

1890 Pierre-Auguste Renoir and Aline Charigot marry on April 14. Monet buys his house in Giverny. On July 27, at Auvers-sur-Oise, Vincent van Gogh shoots himself in the chest with a pistol; he dies two days later.

1883 Durand-Ruel puts Impressionist pictures on view in London; Berlin and Boston both hold major Impressionist exhibitions for the first time.

1884 Joris-Karl Huysmans' novel *À Rebours (Against the Grain)* is published. Les XX group founded in Brussels. First Salon des Indépendants is held in Paris.

1885 Gottlieb Daimler and Wilhelm Maybach construct the first single-cylinder motor vehicle and the first motorcycle to use a gasoline engine.

1886 Eighth Impressionist exhibition. Durand-Ruel shows Impressionist pictures in New York.

1887 In May, Durand-Ruel puts on a second Impressionist exhibition in New York.

1888 Beginning of cooperation between the artists Paul Sérusier, Maurice Denis, and Pierre Bonnard, the later Nabis group.

1889 Fourth Paris World's Fair. Inauguration of the Eiffel Tower.

1892 The Munich Secession is founded.

1895 Ambroise Vollard stages a major exhibition for Cézanne. Wilhelm Röntgen discovers X-rays.

1896 Hugo von Tschudi purchases Impressionist works for the National Gallery, Berlin.

1897 For the first time, the École des Beaux-Arts admits women students. The Vienna Secession is founded.

1898 Thomas Mann publishes his novel *Buddenbrooks*. The Berlin Secession is founded.

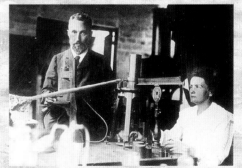

Vincent van Gogh, *Self-Portrait (Dedicated to Paul Gauguin)*, 1889. Oil on canvas, 24½ x 20½ in. (62 x 52 cm). Fogg Art Museum, Harvard University, Cambridge, MA, U.S.

1900 Publication of Sigmund Freud's *The Interpretation of Dreams*.

1901 Serge Diaghilev organizes the first Impressionist exhibition to be held in Russia.

1902 The art historian Julius Meier-Graefe publishes his book *Manet and his Circle*.

1904 Works by Monet, Pissarro, and Renoir on display at the World's Fair in St. Louis, Missouri.

1881 Start of expansionist French policy in Africa.

1882 Introduction of free compulsory primary education in France. Great Britain occupies Egypt.

1883 The Mahdi's rebellion against foreign rule by the British in Sudan. Opening of Brooklyn Bridge in New York, linking Brooklyn and Manhattan.

1885 On February 26, the Berlin Conference on the Congo recognizes the independent Congo State as the private property of the King of Belgium.

1886 The Haymarket Riot in Chicago, Illinois, begins May 1 with a strike lasting several days in support of demands for reduced working hours. Following a bomb explosion, the police use force to restore order.

1887 The new French President, Carnot, endeavors to strengthen ties with Russia, partly through a policy of investment.

1889 The first Pan-American conference is held in Washington, DC, with the aim of securing United States influence in Latin America. Japan adopts a new constitution on the European model.

1892 In Paris, 907 people die of cholera. World's Fair is held in Chicago, Illinois.

1894 First stages of the Dreyfus Affair, which exposes corruption and anti-Semitism in the French army. Outbreak of the Sino-Japanese War.

1896 First Olympic Games of the modern era held in Athens.

1897 First Zionist World Congress held in Basel, Switzerland.

1898 Marie and Pierre Curie discover radium. Zola reaches a wide public with his article defending Dreyfus, a French army officer wrongly convicted of treason.

1900 Fifth Paris World's Fair.

1903 In recognition of their research on radioactivity, the Curies and Henri Becquerel are awarded the Nobel Prize for physics.

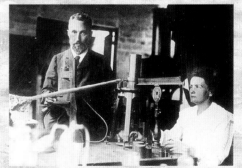

Pierre and Marie Curie, ca. 1900.

Childe Hassam, *Late Afternoon, New York, Winter*, 1900.
Oil on canvas, 37 x 29 in. (94 x 73.7 cm).
Brooklyn Museum of Art, New York.

◁ **Berthe Morisot**, *Eugène Manet and his Daughter in the Garden at Bougival*, 1881. Oil on canvas, 28¾ x 36¼ in. (73 x 92 cm). Private collection.

▷ **Frédéric Bazille**, *View of the Village, Castelnau* (detail), 1868. Oil on canvas, 51¼ x 35 in. (130 x 89 cm). Musée Fabre, Montpellier, France